A First Draft History

The Madison College Experiment in
Christian Education

Written in the Summer of 1912

PERCY T. MAGAN

M. BESSIE DEGRAW

Book design by Eric Koester and Pheonix Hardin
Cover design by Jesús Cordero, Anointing Productions
Typeset with Adobe Caslon 11/13 and Myriad Pro 13

PRINTED IN U.S.A.
ISBN-13: 9780990517535

DEDICATION

To the many men and women who have given all they had to fulfill the mission of the Seventh-day Adventist Church through following the Madison model as outlined in this book.

CONTENTS

All chapters were written by Bessie DeGraw,
unless otherwise noted.

PREFACE

Though Madison College came and went, something about the school and campus still fascinates. The college may have closed in 1964, but people with a serious interest in the mission of the Seventh-day Adventist Church will gravitate to the Madison model and try to apply it to their work, whether it be a school, sanitarium, restaurant, lifestyle center or other self-supporting endeavor. Many just want to see the campus.

The Madison founders proverbially bent over backwards to follow the guidelines of the Ellen White visions at a time when many people were turning them down and going their own way. The divine model called for a school, sanitarium, and farm. Battle Creek College had the school and sanitarium; Emmanuel Missionary College in Berrien Springs, Michigan, had the school and farm, but the Board of Directors there would not add a sanitarium to the complex. Finally, in frustration, prominent educators E.A. Sutherland and Percy T. Magan came south on a self-supporting basis and there brought the divine model for Christian education to full flower. Here, on their own, they could have a farm, school and sanitarium all in one unit, as they called the enterprise.

This model has stood the test of time. Excellent people have run and staffed other Adventist colleges and universities, but none have been as memorable as that little school on the banks of the Cumberland River a few miles out of Nashville, Tennessee.

Sutherland and Magan, along with the students and teachers working under them, did all they could to follow the Lord's directions as given through the divine inspiration of Ellen White, though it did not fully agree with their initial plans, even to the point of choosing a spot on the farm for the sanitarium.

In so doing, they knew they were making history, having seen what had happened back in Battle Creek when smart, educated people disregarded Ellen White when her counsel diverged from their own good ideas.

This book presents a thorough account of the Madison experiment fresh in their minds eight years after starting out anew in Tennessee and can serve as a guide to all wanting educational reform.

I found this typewritten manuscript in the archives of the Layman Foundation headquarters in Collegedale, Tennessee. Some of the type was hard to read, having been in storage for so long, and I was forced to delete some sentences because I was unable to decipher key words. But the message still comes through loud and clear.

I wish to thank Eric Koester of the Adventist Digital Library for providing me with computer software to scan this document on screen and transcribe it to readability, and also Larry Ashcraft for making the Highland Academy computer lab available to me with equipment that was able to handle the software necessary to transcribe. I otherwise would have had to enter it into a computer by hand.

This booklet will thus inspire those pressing for reform in preparation for the Second Coming.

Albert Dittes
Portland, Tennessee
August 1, 2017

The text that follows is a faithful transcription of the original rough draft. Grammatical and typographical idiosyncrasies, as well as various redundancies, reflect the work of the original authors.

CHAPTER 1

THE BIRTH OF THE MADISON MODEL

By Percy T. Magan

Probably not all Institutions have a prenatal history, but the Nashville Agricultural and Normal Institute (N.A.N.I.) has one; and, as is frequently the case in human lives, the prenatal influence was most influential in shaping the life of the institution. Not all institutions can be said to possess a parent, but the N.A.N.I. had a mother. It did not spring full-grown from the head of some Greek Zeus, as some institutions appear to have done, but came into the world as a babe brought forth with much travail of soul, called into existence by the voice of God and given a mission as distinct and convincing as ever was given to Jeremiah or Hosea.

The mother institution was Battle Creek College, the pride for many long years of every loyal Seventh-day Adventist. Within her walls the principles and policies were shaped which are like the formation of bone and sinew in the unborn infant. Forces were at work there which baffled understanding, truly as nature herself baffles understanding when she produces new seed from the old kernel or a new being from matter already in existence.

It is not wise to dwell too long on still-before-birth history, for the beginning of education reform in Battle Creek College is well-known. In the early history of that institution, an attempt was made to combine manual and intellectual culture. The institution's history might easily be compared in this respect to the history of other well-known schools, such as the University of Virginia in its early days.

The Spirit of Prophecy had said from the beginning that every school should be on a farm. Battle Creek College, when located, was surrounded by considerable open country, but the town grew up to the school. Various industries were from time to time made a part of the regular college curriculum, but the influence of other state institutions was strong, and gradually the industries were eliminated. There were various attempts at reform, always in the direction of making the education more practical.

It was at last realized that if young men and women were to be trained as they should be for the mission fields, opportunity should be afforded for the cultivation of the soil. A farm was purchased about a mile north of the college campus, and here a certain class of students were given an opportunity to work their way through school and at the same time to study the principles of agriculture. In this way, the first move was made by these educators to combine college work with the cultivation of the soil. The attempt was unsuccessful for various reasons. The farm was in one place, the school in another; and the conditions separated the class of students who worked on the farm from those in other sections of the school.

The next attempt to combine the industries with college work came in the year 1901, when Battle Creek College was moved from its original site to Berrien Springs, Michigan. This school was located on a 270-acre farm, and on this farm was built up an institution where, in better circumstances, could be carried out the ideals in education outlined to Seventh-day Adventists by the Bible and the Spirit of Prophecy. In that farm school were taught some of the great questions of denominational education. There great victories were won, especially along the following lines: manual education should be deemed of equal importance with mental culture; the two united, equalized, balanced, deserve the term cultural education. Self-support by students is possible; where industries are taught and self-support is made possible, self-government must follow as thunder follows lightning, or as one foot follows the other in walking.

The men and women who began this educational reform had many lessons to learn. They themselves had been educated according to the old system of education. It was the idea that the classroom teacher stood on one plane, while the industrial worker occupied a place a little below. The first effort at Berrien Springs was to elevate industrial education and industrial workers to a level with purely intellectual culture. To do this, each member of the faculty was expected to participate in the two lines of work. That was one great step in the direction of reform. Students were given an opportunity to work to meet their school expenses, making it necessary to equalize as far as possible the amount of time spent in industrial work and in classroom work. A student, to be self-supporting, must spend at least one-half of the day in manual work; the other half could be devoted to study and classroom work. It was with this idea in mind that the one-study plan was adopted at Berrien Springs. Where the industries are taught and self-support is made possible, self-government naturally follows. This led to a development of a system of cooperation between teachers and students in the work of the institution.

The truth of these propositions was established at Berrien Springs, but it remained for the new school, the child of that, to develop them and present them in working form to those, both in the world and in the religious organization, who are seeking some tangible proof of their possibility. The story of their development is an interesting one, and it is around this story that the history of the institution centers. Rather, it is the development of these principles that forms the history of this institution.

Not all who had part in the work at Berrien Springs were equally interested in the development of reforms. Some felt that they could go further than others. Conditions there were to a degree restrictive, and circumstances so shaped themselves that those who were more progressive in spirit felt it would be wise to establish a new school under still more favorable conditions.

For a number of years, the South had been a field studied by instructors and teachers in Berrien Springs and Battle Creek. Some of the workers in those institutions had spent time in the South and were familiar with various lines of work being carried on by the Southern Missionary Society and other organizations. Students had been encouraged to go south to enter the work. Canvassers from the school had been sent into this field. The work needed among the mountaineers of the South had been studied, and there had been quite a deep interest aroused among students at Berrien Springs.

It was decided, therefore, by several of the Berrien Springs workers in the spring of 1904, to sever their connection with that institution and begin a quiet work in the South. It was at first their purpose to locate in some mountain section and establish a small mountain school. There was but a limited amount of money at the command of this company, and the school was to be built and conducted within the bounds of their finances.

Views of Nashville Agricultural and Normal Institute, circa 1912

CHAPTER 2

MAKING THE PURCHASE

A trip was made to Nashville by Brethren Sutherland and Magan. By invitation they joined Elder J. E. White's company, composed of Sister E. G. White, Elder W. C. White, and others, who were going up the Cumberland in the steamer "Morning Star." Sister White herself, writing to Elder Daniells in a letter dated June 13, 1904, speaks of this trip as follows:

> We are returning from our trip up the river to look for land suitable for school work. We went from Nashville to Carthage, a distance of about 170 miles by the river and 78 miles by rail. We looked at several places; but the fertile land up the river is altogether too high in price for us to think of purchasing it for school purposes.
>
> Tomorrow morning (June 14) we shall reach Edgefield Junction, which is only 1 miles from Nashville. We shall stay there for the rest of the day; for we wish to visit a farm which is for sale near Madison about nine miles from Nashville, and two and a half miles from the railway. It is said that this farm contains nearly 100 acres of good bottom land, more than 100 acres of second quality agricultural land suitable for grain and fruit, and about 200 acres of pasture land. We think that it can be purchased for about $12,000. It is said that there is on it over $2,000 worth of stock and farm implements. I desire to look at this farm, and if it be the will of the Lord, I shall do so tomorrow afternoon. The farm has a roomy house, barns and other buildings, and two and a half miles of good stone fence. Considering its advantages, its price is less than anything else we have seen in this part of Tennessee.

On the boat, Sister White talked with the two brethren concerning their future school. After listening to the plans for a little mountain school, she said, "Your plans are too narrow. God would have a larger work done. Nashville has often been pointed out to me as a city that should be entered by our people. A school should be established near Nashville where workers can be trained to start just such little schools as you have described. The Lord has shown me that this should be done."

Immediately after the Berrien Springs Council, Sister White, went South with Edson, and our idea was that we wouldn't go for two months yet. That was the 21st of May 1904. I was to visit camp meetings, and then we were going, Sutherland and I, for our ride in Virginia. She no sooner got there than she telegraphed for us to come. We went down. She was stopping with J. E. out in that old wooden building that is now the publishing house. When we went in, she said, "Brother Magan and Brother Sutherland, I thought I should like to know a little more about your plans."

Well, we told her we were going off into a quiet place by ourselves, take what little money we could scrape up between us—which would be in single figures in the thousands—we would get a little place and get two or three students, build up a very quiet little work for the mountaineers, and earn a living with our own hands off the soil. We would never have run a big place like this; a training school was not in our heads at all. We were sick of fighting and quarreling—and probably as much to blame as anyone else—we would dig a living out of the dirt, and let it go.

She says, "Yes, that's what was shown me. And that is why I telegraphed for you; because that's all wrong."

She told us she had been shown that plan was all wrong, and that after we had had fifteen or twenty years' experience in the work, the Lord would be displeased if we went off by ourselves, and that we were to start a larger work and a training work in proximity to the other institutions. We told her we did not have money enough to do that, and as things were, we did not know whether we could get any help. She talked about our having faith, and the Lord would raise up friends. So we told her we would look for a place around here.

Then Prof. Sutherland and I started in to hunt for a place. We stayed with Will Palmer. He loaned us a horse. But we did not seem to strike any place that suited us. Then one day someone told Will Palmer about this place. Prof. Sutherland, I think, had gone back to Nashville. I drove over here one morning with Will and saw it. We thought it was a very cheap place. They wanted $12,000, with everything on it: cattle, mules, machinery, wagons, single buggy, harnesses, tools, and the growing crop. I wasn't stuck enough on the place to impress me very much, but Will Palmer told Sister White about it. And from the very first she heard of it, she seemed to be settled on it. When I came down to Nashville she talked to me about it, and asked me if I had seen that big place on the river for sale.

"What do you think of it?" she asked.

"Just as little as I can help," I said, "It's too big a place, it's rocky, it takes more money than we have."

She says, "Well, I'm sorry, because it seems to me that is the place."

Prof. Sutherland came and looked at it with me then, and he didn't like it. Sister White had been talking to him about it, and he sort of blamed me for putting her up to it. The next thing was the river trip. J. E. was going to take Sister White around to show her the South, and of course he had to do it on the boat. Then he didn't know but what somewhere upstream he would get a farm to start a Negro training school.

She got on the boat one night, and I was to join them the next day at Edgefield, Sutherland too, perhaps. At any rate, the boat was to reach Edgefield at noon the next day. But it was six o'clock before the boat got there. When I walked over the gangplank Halladay says, "We broke down today."

"Yes, I says, "your old shebang is always breaking down; that's nothing new." He says, "We broke down off that place on the river, and Sister White went up and looked at it."

"Just like your crazy boat to break down where we don't want her to," I said.

Then Will pipes up, "And mother would like to see you in the cabin, please, Brother Magan."

I went in; I think Sutherland was with me. She says, "Well, Brother Magan, I saw your farm to-day, and I walked all over it, and I'm much convinced that is the place God wants you to have. It's the kind of place that has been shown me."

I said, "All right, Mother; if that is the way you feel about it, we'll see what we can do."

17

She said, "Yes, I feel that way about it."

Ed and I went out and down to the stern of that boat and sat down on the wheel. We sat there till one or two o'clock in the morning, chewing that thing over and abusing our luck. We had decided we would come south; that was as big a thing as we thought we could undertake; a little quiet place was big enough, and now we were driven off into this place, expensive and unattractive. At three o'clock we settled that we had better do it, because we were put up to it by the testimony.

The whole way up the river she could talk about nothing else but this place. We got off at Hartsville, as well as at other places, and had big times. Nothing else interested her. At College (Carthage) J. E. was going to Paducah; she would not go: "Turn around and let me see that place again!"

We came back and walked into the dock at Edgefield. Will Palmer's and J. E.'s rigs were there. She, Will, J. E., and Sarah drove over here. Ed and I felt so blue we would not go, but we drove on down the bend to the old Ford place. We came out and looked it over once more, and sat out on that sheet of rock west of Mrs. Druillard's cottage. Ed doesn't very often shed tears, but he cried as if his heart would break. He said, "It's the roughest, weediest, most miserable thing I've ever seen, and it does me up and makes me sick, the whole thought of it!" and he blamed me. Thought I had started her off on the tangent. But we decided there was nothing to do but take it.

We arranged, I think, to meet Ferguson, the man who owned it, down in Nashville. We met him in Bennett's Livery. Up there in the loft of that livery we talked with him and made a bargain with him, and paid him five dollars to make out a contract to take the place. I think in one way or another we had scraped together about $1,000 or $1,500. He agreed to take $12,000 for the whole place, including all the cattle—a lot of good fat cattle, wildest steers you ever laid eyes on—-and the mules, old Rhody and Henry and Dey, and Nellie the mare. Then he would make us a donation back (didn't want his wife to know) of $200.

Every time we told Sister White we didn't like it, because it was poor and rocky, and so forth, and wouldn't such and such a place be nicer, she would say, "That's just the way Daniells talked about Cooranbong! That's just the way Daniells talked!"

Ed went north that night on the train, and I was to come over here the next day and draw up the contract with him and sign it. The next day I came and met old Ferguson out by the well. The first thing he said was, "Well, Professor, I'm afraid all our time has been for nothing. Miss Sallie will not sell this place; I'm ashamed, but I can't help it."

I says, "What's the matter with Miss Sallie?"

"I hate to tell you," he says, "but she says that a damned Yankee shall never own this place."

I said, "You let me see her. We have bargained with you; my friends have gone; you have put us to a lot of expense, and you lay yourselves liable to a suit." I tried to persuade him and I tried to scare him.

"I don't think you would better see her," he says. "When Miss Sallie gets on a tantrum, she acts like the very devil."

I said, "Maybe, but I've talked to women that acted like the devil more than once."

Well, he took me in, into the lower room on the south; it was her parlor, very nicely fixed up. I was sitting in there, when he came into the room: a great tall fellow, and she, taller yet, right behind him. I have often pictured Jezebel in my mind; and I thought I surely saw her on that trip. He says, "Miss Sallie, I want to introduce you to Professor Magan."

She turned on him, stamped her foot, and hissed, "You get out of the room, Sir!" He got. Then she turned to me, "And now, Sir, what may you want?"

I said, "Miss Sallie, if you'll sit down and be quiet a minute, I'll talk to you."

She dropped into a chair, just as floppy as Miss DeGraw there.

"Now," I said, "your husband tells me that you don't want to sell the place. You have put us into a pretty hard place, because you have agreed to sell it. My friends have gone now..."

She says, "I'll never sell this place to a damned Yankee!"

"You might sell it to an Irishman, wouldn't you?" I said. "I don't own there's any Yankee in me."

She just sat there, looking as hard and devilish, and all she said, her own words, "I won't have anything to do with the damned Yankees!"

I don't know what impulse in me made me say it, but I suddenly said. "Miss Sallie, were you ever a Christian?"

And the tears came right up into her eyes the minute I said it and fell down her face. She burst into uncontrollable tears, and said, "Oh, I used to be. My father was a Methodist minister, and he brought me up to be a Christian woman; but it just seems to me as if the very devil has gotten into me."

I said, "That's what your husband told me. Now, Miss Sallie, if the Lord does not want us to have this place, we don't want it. Let's kneel down on our knees and ask the Lord to show us this thing right."

She cried as if her heart would break, and down on our knees we got, Miss Sallie and I, and we prayed. I prayed the Lord to take the devil out of her, and she prayed the same thing; told Him she knew she had the devil in her and she wanted Him to take him out. When we got up from our knees, her face was radiant! "You draw up that contract," she said. "I'll go and help Laura and the girls get the luncheon, and you draw up the contract, and then you come in and eat, and after that I'll go over the papers with you, and I'll sign."

So I got to work on the contract, and after awhile she came, just as nice as pie, and called me to dinner. We ate dinner and chatted along. When we got up, she went away upstairs. I went back into the parlor, and I said, "Now, Mr. Ferguson, I'm all ready, so we'll sign up."

He went upstairs and didn't come down for half an hour, and I felt the heavens were getting black. When he came down, he says, "Professor, it's all off again. It's no good; she's just acting like hell! The girls are up there beseeching her, but it's no good." (She had several grown daughters and some sons.)

"Well," I said, "get her down again."

"No," he says, "it's no use."

"It is use," I said, "get her down; because we are going to have this place."

"How do you know that?" he asked.

"It wouldn't do any good to tell you how I know it," I said, "but I know it. Get her down."

Well, after half an hour she came down, and we sat on the porch and we talked back and forth, and she told me how she hated the Yankees. She knew the Lord or something had touched her when we prayed, but she was off again, and it was no good. I told her I was going to keep on calling

20

on her until we got the turn. She wanted to sell the place, and she didn't want to, she wanted to and she didn't, and so it went.

I telegraphed Prof. Sutherland that night and told him to come down again, because we would evidently have to pay more, and it was a question whether we would get this place or get something else; whichever way, he and Mrs. Druillard ought to be here.

While they were coming down, she said, "Do you want the place?"

We said, "Yes, we have decided to take that option."

She said, "I don't know whether I'll sign it now or not, but if I were in Nashville I think I would."

I took her by the arm and hopped her into a buggy we had there, and started for town, Ed and I and she and Henry, her son. She was in that frame of mind; wanted to, but couldn't. We got her downtown and into the notary's office. Under Tennessee law a married woman is not a woman; she is simply non fam., under the old Latin law. It is both a good thing and a bad thing; she can break her word and you can't do a thing to her. If a deed is signed jointly by a man and his wife, the woman must go into a room with a notary public, apart from her husband or any of her kin, and take an oath that she is not being coerced, etc.

She signed the deed, and then it came to that oath. Ferguson and all the rest went out of the room. I stayed there with the notary public. She said, "I'll never sign that; I'm not doing this thing freely."

He said, "You do as you please, Madam; I'm not going to take your oath unless you do."

She stopped and bit her lip, white as a sheet. "The damned Yankees! The damned Yankees!" she said under her breath; that was all she could say.

Her brother came into the room. He said, Oh Sallie, do quit that."

She said, "They have got to pay me in gold."

"No," he said, "their check is all right."

Finally she turned to the notary, and said, "I subscribe to that oath, Sir. Give me the pen."

She took her pen and scribbled her name. By that time, we had enough money to make the payment: five thousand plus a great deal of it borrowed money. I handed her a check for the $5,000, and Ed and I stuck those papers in our pockets, and we got out of the house as fast as we could and went down and filed them before she could change her mind.

That night we went in to see Sister White, and Ed says, "Well, Mother, we have the place."

She said, "Well, Brother Sutherland, you boys will never know how many angels worked to help you get it."

You know all the time I had been thinking, while I was fooling with that old Jezebel, about those words in the book of Daniel, where Gabriel told him he would have come sooner, but he had to resist . . . and all the time it was coming to my mind an angel was fighting for us.

Then we said, "Mother, why did you want us so much to have that place? It's back of beyond-and-why, and the rocks are so thick on it they can't lie down flat. We bought it and it's all right, but we have done it just because of your word."

She says, "Well, brethren, whom did you come down here to help?"

"Oh, we came to help these poor people in the hills."

"And do you think it would be becoming for you to have the best piece of land in the state so as to fit yourselves for laboring among these people who have this very poor land in the hills?"

We began to see light; we told her we saw that. Then we tackled her about the money.

"Well now," she says, "the Lord has led you men through some hard places and given you great experiences, and if you trust Him, you will have some more. You will get the money, and I will help you. I will write something, and I will put it in the Review."

"Well, but," Ed says, "the brethren won't want us to get any."

She says. "You leave them to me; I'll tend to them."

So then we got George Alcorn down here, or Brink first, and we both went back up to Berrien Springs. We had that meeting in the grove and talked things over, and students decided to come with us. Years ago, the Spirit of Prophecy stated, "The Lord is grieved by the woe in the southern field. Christ has wept at the sight of this woe. Angels have hushed the music of their harps as they have looked upon a people unable to help themselves." They decided they would throw in their lot with us, whether we got anything or not. No one was to have any pay, or any promise of anything more than what there was. Alcorn and Brink were here in the summer; Mrs. Sutherland and Joe came in August.

CHAPTER 3

AN EXCERPT FROM THE REVIEW AND HERALD

Concerning this part of the history, Sister White herself wrote [the following] in the Review and Herald of August 1, 1904.

In connection with the work in Nashville, I wish to speak of the school work that Brethren Sutherland and Magan are planning to do. I was surprised when, in speaking of the work they wished to do in the South, they spoke of establishing a school in some place a long way from Nashville. From the light given me, I know that this would not be the right thing to do, and I told them so. The work that these brethren can do, because of the experience gained at Berrien Springs, is to be carried on within easy access of Nashville; for Nashville has not yet been worked as it should be. And it will be a great blessing to the workers in the school to be near enough to Nashville to be able to counsel with the workers there.

In searching for a place for the school, the brethren found a farm of 400 acres for sale, about nine miles from Nashville. The size of the farm, its situation, the distance that it is from Nashville, and the moderate sum for which it could be purchased, seemed to point it out as the very place for the school work. We advised that this place be purchased. I knew that all the land would ultimately be needed. For the work of the students, and to provide homes for the teachers, such land can be used advantageously. And as our work advances, a portion of this tract may be required for a country sanitarium.

Other properties were examined, but we found nothing so well suited for our work. The price of the place, including standing crops, farm machinery, and over 70 head of cattle, was $12,723. It has been purchased, and as soon as possible, Brethren Magan and Sutherland, with a few experienced helpers, will begin school work there. We feel confident that the Lord has been guiding in this matter.

The plan upon which our brethren propose to work is to select some of the best and most substantial young men and women from Berrien Springs and other places in the North; we believe that God has called them to the work in the South, and give them a brief training as teachers. Thorough instruction will be given in Bible study, physiology, and the history of our message; and special instruction in agriculture will be given. It is hoped that many of these students will eventually connect with schools in various places in the South. In connection with these schools, there will be land that will be cultivated by teachers and students, and the proceeds from this work will be used for the support of the schools.

We went once more to see the farm, after its purchase had been completed, and were very much pleased with it. I earnestly hope that the school to be established there will be a success, and will help to build up the work of the Lord in that part of the vineyard. There are men of means in various parts of the land who can assist this enterprise by loans without interest and by liberal gifts.

Let us sustain Brethren Sutherland and Magan in their efforts to advance this important work. They gained a valuable experience in Berrien Springs, and the providence of God has led them to feel that they must labor in the southern field. God helped them constantly in their efforts at Berrien Springs, as they steadily advanced, determined that obstacles should not stop the work. They are not leaving Berrien Springs because of dissension or strife. They are not fleeing from duty. They are leaving a place where a school has been established to go to a new field, where the work may be much harder. They have only means enough to pay part of the price of the land. They should not be left to struggle along, misunderstood and unaided, at the sacrifice of health.

As these brethren go to the South to take hold of pioneer work in a difficult field, we ask our people to make their work as effective as possible by assisting then in the establishment of the new school near Nashville.

I ask our people to help the work in the southern field by aiding Brethren Sutherland and Magan and their faithful associates in the carrying forward of the important enterprise they have undertaken. Brethren and sisters, the poverty and the needs of the southern field call urgently for your assistance. There is a great work to be done in that field, and we ask you to act your part.

CHAPTER 4

SMALL BEGINNINGS

Possession was to be given the first of October, but there was stock on the place, and crops that required attention. At a council that was held at Berrien Springs. Students and teachers talked over the new southern proposition. A number of students signified their desire to become associated with the new movement. Among these were Brethren Chas. F. Alden, O. A. Wolcott, Calvin Kinsman, George Alcorn (and wife), Ernest Dunn, E. E. Brink, and the Misses Shannon, Ashton, and Abegg.

About the first of July the advance guard left Michigan for Nashville, Tennessee. Bro. Elmer Brink and Bro. Ernest Bunn came to look after the stock on the farm. A little later Bro. George Alcorn Joined them. In August, Mrs. Sutherland, with her five-month-old baby, and Miss Shannon and Miss Abegg, reached Nashville. A little later Bro. Alcorn's wife joined the company.

Bro. George Alcorn put up a small cottage, which was the first new building on the place. Bro. Brink took the oversight of the stock, and the first churning in the future institution was done by him in a little lean-to on the north side of the Old Plantation House. In fact, for a year after this institution was launched, this same lean-to was the only creamery, but from it came sweet, pure butter, the first visible means of self-support for the little company.

Through the trying heat of that August the women of the company occupied a room in the former Negro quarters of the horse barn, with the driving horse and the buggies on the first floor. They were not permitted even to sit on the spacious porch of the Plantation House, so persistent was the ire of the woman who lived in the house. The sod about the old Plantation House pastured the calves, the colts, the geese, and the ducks, until practically not a spear of grass was allowed to grow during the dry season. The hogs wallowed just outside the stone fence of the compound.

In August, Bro. Alcorn built the first cottage of the institution, a little two-room house now known as Ames Cottage, occupied by Bro. Kendall and family so long as he retained his connection with the school as farm manager, and later by students attending the school with families.

The first of October 1904, Old Plantation House was vacated by the former owners, and the school company moved in. The moving in was a simple affair. A few spring cots and some chairs were purchased, a board on four feet of a dry-goods box made a washstand, and up to the present time, relics of that primitive furniture can be found. Eight or nine people gathered about the first table. One picture indelibly printed on the mind of one of those first few, shows Mrs. Druillard, as master of the inn, morning by morning slaughtering flies while they were still stiff from the cool of the night. With her years of experience in home institutions and in foreign fields, she was yet not above standing at the forefront of a pioneer movement and taking the hard side of things as they came. Her spirit of courage, her trust in the Lord, and her wise economy helped steer this frail bark over a tempestuous sea. And as late as 1912, eight years after the founding, she is still the mother of the institution, the leading spirit in the rural sanitarium which came into existence in due order of things, and she is still the same efficient business manager.

CHAPTER 5

FOUNDATION STONES LAID

A company of workers that looks for success must counsel often. As soon as one member acts independently of the rest, dissatisfaction will arise. The founders of the Nashville Agricultural and Normal Institute knew this to be true, and the annals of the institution show that scarcely three weeks from the date when possession was taken of the property, the first meeting of founders (which was then a name applied to all on the place, irrespective of age, position, or previous calling) was called to outline a policy. From the minutes of that first meeting, the following paragraphs are quoted as showing the problems the little company had then to deal with—the financial question, etc.:

UNION MEETING

Held Sunday, September 3, 1905, at 7:30 P.M.,

in the chapel , the southwest room of Old Plantation.

E.A. Sutherland in the chair.

Brother Brink was called on for a report concerning the cattle, and stated that he thought they could get along without ground feed for the present, as the water supply is good.

The question of a proper place for the chicken park was introduced by Mr. Austin. The body seemed unable to take a position in regard to it, and it was voted that the question be tabled for one week.

The grindstone, Mr. Kinsman stated, has been spoiled for fine work, and files are also needed for sharpening building tools. This matter was left open.

Some kind of pump will be needed in a very few days. It was voted on motion of C. F. Alden that a committee of two be appointed from the floor to consider the pump question and report Monday evening.

C. D. Kinsman and E. A. Sutherland were appointed.

The Chair brought up the matter of a new barn, and it was voted, on motion of C. D. Kinsman, seconded by C. F. Alden, that a committee of three be appointed from the floor to study this problem and report plans at the next weekly meeting, or sooner if possible.

The persons named on this committee were K. F. Brink, C. F. Alden, and S. P. Austin.

The case of Ernest Houpt was discussed. It was a question whether a nurse could be procured for him or he should be sent to the Sanitarium, but action was postponed, awaiting the arrival of Dr. Magan.

The matter of irregularities and reporting the same was discussed by Brother Alden and Professor Sutherland. No action was taken, as the hour was late, and the matter was left over for further consideration.

Meeting adjourned.

M. Bessie DeGraw, Secretary.

At an irregular meeting during the week, the Committee on Cottage Building offered the following recommendation, which was adopted:

...that a two-room cottage be built between the Alcorn and the Sutherland cottages, 32 x 12, with a back porch, the style to be similar to that of the Priscilla. The foundation is to have pillars instead of a stone wall. The walls are to have sheeting and paper, and to be plastered, and the cottage is to have double floor. M. B. D..

The record shows that five meetings were held during the remaining days of October. During that time steps were taken which have never been retraced. A few of these are worthy of notice.

CHAPTER 6

WAGES

A committee was appointed to study this question. It brought in the following recommendations, which were adopted. It was thought by those who agreed to this plan that for $13.00 a month per worker to cover board, room, fuel, laundry, etc. they could manage with the clothing they then had, plus the little money they might individually command, to live that way for one year. At the end of the first year, when the financial report was rendered, it was found that the small income from the farm had largely gone into the support of students who came for an education and were given work, but who had little or no cash to put into school expenses.

And so in October 1905, when the second school year began, it was decided to continue the $13 per month wage to teachers, and still "to discourage any from connecting with the work as teachers who could not get along in this way."

Eight years have now passed. Some of that original number have left to go into the work elsewhere, as the further reading of this history shows, and others have from time to time been added to the faculty, but the plan of payment has not yet changed, Each year it is studied; each year it is hoped that the income will be sufficient to raise the salary of these faithful laborers, and yet it remains true that while the farm shows a gain of a few hundred dollars each year, it has never been deemed sufficient, in view of the students who need help, to raise the wage.

Can men maintain themselves and their families on $13 per month? That question, so often asked, is always answered in the negative. No member of the Nashville Agricultural and Normal Institute faculty would endeavor to carry that idea, but the original plan has been adhered to. Donations to the institution are not used for food nor for salary. Some of the workers come south with a small income, which has clothed them. Some have been helped by friends and relatives. God has opened unthought-of avenues to those who went into this work without reserve. A number of those who have had a part in the school were able to stay only a year or so. Some have gone out for a time to earn money to enable them to maintain their place in the school. Luke says that in the ministry of Christ and his apostle, "certain women . . . ministered unto him of their substance." Both men and women have been led by the Spirit of God to minister unto this work in various ways and at different times.

CHAPTER 7

FACULTY STUDIES

S carcely was the name faculty applicable, before plans were laid for regular studies. The first ones suggested were educational conditions in the South, how to make the farm pay, crops to raise, how to get money for furniture and machinery, etc. And from that day to the present the faculty meetings of the N.A.N.S. have differed from those in many institutions.

There has been no sitting on cases of discipline.

The faculty is relieved of that work by the Union Body. But hours have been spent over the study of methods on how to make the work more efficient, how to reach more people with the South's need, how to improve the land, the dairy herd, the best way to save the orchard from disease and destroying pests, how to furnish remunerative work for boys in bad weather, etc. etc. The unity that these studies bring is due in large measure to the success of the little company.

Tree planting ceremony, circa 1912.

CHAPTER 8

UNION MEETINGS

By the first of November 1904, several students had been added to the family, and Union Meetings were organized. It was the purpose of the Founders to develop to the fullest extent possible the spirit of Christian democracy. The Union Body was comprised of teachers and students. It was made the legislative body of the school. It also had executive power. We are told

> Cooperation should be the spirit of the schoolroom, the law of its life.
>
> Education, p. 285.

> The rules governing the schoolroom should, so far as possible, represent the voice of the school. Every principle involved in them should be so plainly before the student that he may be convinced of its justice. Thus he will feel a responsibility to see that the rules which he himself has helped to frame shall be enforced.
>
> Ibid., p. 290.

It was for the purpose of obeying this instruction, deemed divine, and further exemplified in the life of Moses, that the Union Body was organized. From that day to the present the Union Body has existed. It has grown from a dozen members to nearly 70, but scarcely a week has passed in eight years without a meeting of this body. It has been one of the strongest single educational factors in the life of the school. Through it, each student is kept in touch with the workings of every department of the institution. In it is developed thought, ability to speak in public, the power of initiative, referendum, and recall, the things the democratic world now clamors for.

Practically all the rules governing the school have been made in the open session of the Union Body. It is the custom to study the Spirit of Prophecy and the Bible for principles to direct in the work, and then to formulate rules in harmony with these principles. The student body divides itself naturally into two divisions. There is the men's department, which considers practically all the work done for the institution that is carried on by the men. In the women's department, the work done by women students and teachers is considered. These bodies formulate rules governing their departments, present them to the Union Body, where they are discussed, possibly amended, sometimes rejected, and sometimes accepted; but when once accepted, they become part of the governing laws of the school. Rules formulated in this way are posted on the bulletin board, and each member of the school is expected to abide by the rules of the body. The majority rules. The man who happens to be in the minority is expected to abide by the rules of the majority until such a time as he is able to convince the body of some wiser course.

CHAPTER 9

WORSHIP

From the day of its birth, the institution has had worship both morning and evening. At first it was held about the open fireplace in the dining room of Old Plantation, the chapped hands of the boys being doctored betimes by Mother D. They husked corn in the chill air, and she healed their wounds with bran poultices. Morning worship is still held immediately after breakfast, when everybody drops his work unless it be the nurse who is caring for the sick, and the family gathers in Gotzian Hall for song, prayer and Scripture study. Each evening, when the chores are done and classwork is over, the family again meet in the same place, this time for a longer hour. Once a week the time is taken for Union Meeting, and once more for students' prayer service. Friday evening it is for a vesper social meeting. Saturday evening, in pleasant weather, it is a song service with the patients at the Sanitarium. Once each week, throughout the greater part of the history of the school, an evening has been spent in the study of current history. The first reference to this study is found in the minutes of October 15, 1905, "VOTED, That Monday evening each week be devoted to a study of current topics."

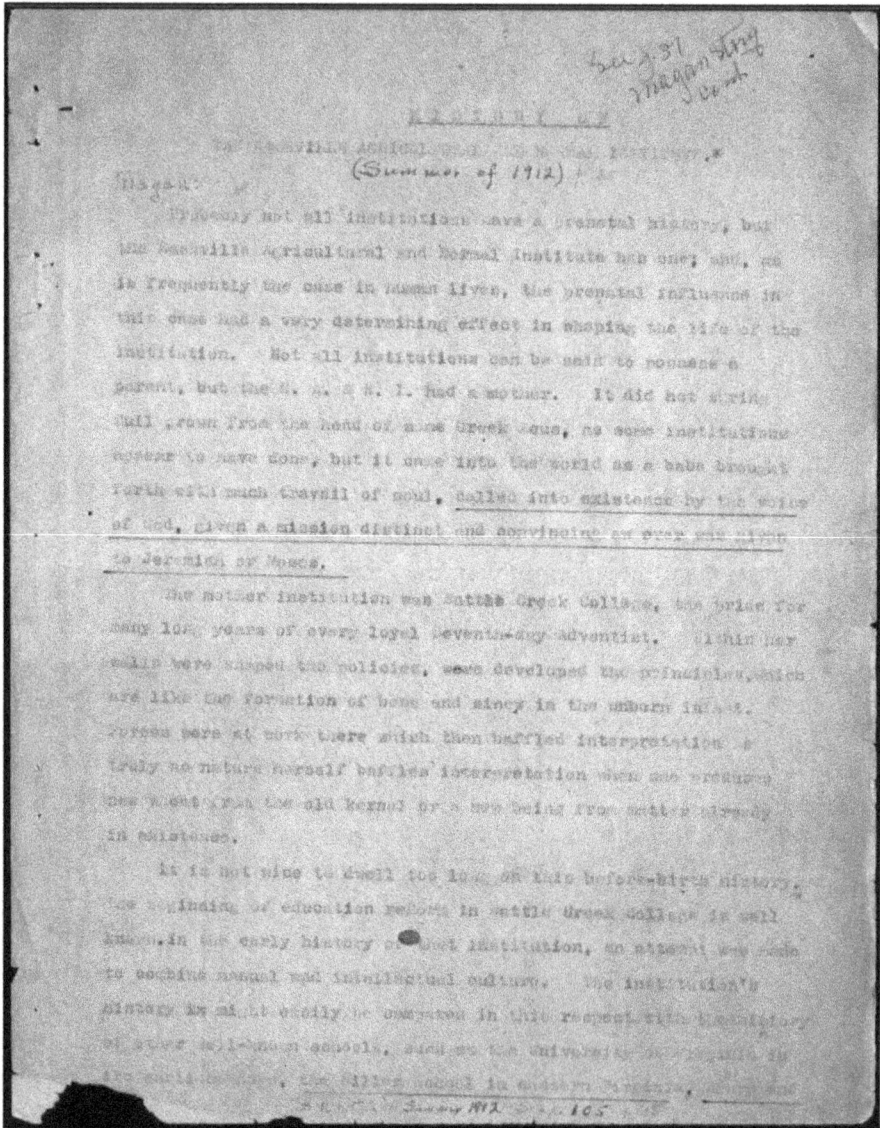

*The first page of this manuscript as it was found in
the Layman Foundation archives.*

CHAPTER 10

LIBRARY

Chapel in those early days was held in the front room of Old Plantation, a room twenty feet square, with nine-foot ceiling, two windows and two doors, an open fireplace, seated with willow-bottom chairs—dark and poorly ventilated, but the only place available for chapel and classwork. The library consisted of a few shelves of plain lumber placed in one corner. The books were donated from the private libraries of founders and by friends who from time to time have generously sent supplies. Among the donors should be numbered Mr. Edgar Nelton of Battle Creek, who has kindly furnished a number of books; Mrs. E. G. White, who supplied the Nashville Agricultural and Normal Institute, as well as the auxiliary schools, with copies of her works; and the Pacific Press and Review & Herald; also Bro. Charles Hobbs, who sent a complete set of Encyclopedia Britannica.

In this connection it is well to say that from that bookshelf in the dark corner, the library gradually emerged, after a transitional period in Phelps Hall to its present quarters in Gotzian Hall, in what is known as the Marian Davis Reading Room. Sister Marian Davis, for many years Sr. White's editorial assistant, remembered the N.A.N.I. in her will, and the gift is commemorated in the present library room.

A reading table has been maintained from the day when the Union body voted to study current history. In it are found the denominational papers, a daily paper, and copies of various leading periodicals, such as the Literary Digest, World's Work, Review of Reviews, etc., and a representative periodical for each of various industries represented in the work of the institution, such as the farm, dairy, garden, sheep-raising, blacksmithing, carpentry, mechanics, nursing, domestic science, etc. The family bears a monthly tax to cover expenses of these periodicals.

Ellen G. White posing with personal staff and the administrators of the college.

Back row: Clarence Crisler, Percy Magan,
Minnie Crisler, Nellie Druillard,
Edward Sutherland, Sarah McEnterfer

Front row: W. C. White, Ellen White,
Emma White, Edson White

Right: An enlarged view of Percy Magan.

CHAPTER 11

TWO HOUR TIME

Each calendar that is issued mentions the fact that each member of the family is asked to put in two hours' work per day without remuneration. This custom, still prevailing, dates back to those early meetings in October 1904. About the institution there is a large general expense such as office work, handling mail, caring for lawns, telephone services, general wear and tear that cannot be met by donations, and it does not fall legitimately into any one department. It was agreed to cooperate by working two hours per day to cover this. This is not a tuition charge, as is sometimes thought. The institution gives free tuition. It shuts no one from its doors who seeks an education and who is willing to work, but the family unites in bearing a burden not otherwise provided for by this two-hour plan.

First Draft History

CHAPTER 12

EQUIPMENT

The equipment came slowly. The following statement from the minutes of meetings of the Union Body tells the story:

Nov. 12, 1904. "Mrs. Druillard stated that when the steers are sold, a cream separator can he purchased,"

Nov. 19. "Mr. Wolcott was asked to order a 450-pound Sharpies separator through his uncle."

Nov. 27. "It was voted to keep the separator in the back hallway of Old Plantation until a more suitable place is provided."

Later it was moved into the laundry, where it stood until the present small separator house was built in the fall of 1905, near the barns.

The evolution of the idea of laundry and bathrooms is shown in the following:

Nov. 27, 1904. "The advisability of building a small house that will serve as a bathroom and wash-house was discussed. Mrs. Druillard advised using the little cook house (a little shack built by Bro. Brink and Bro. Dunn before the company took possession of the place—now gone), and thought the expenditure of $100 ought to put it in shape."

This plan failed to carry, and a committee was appointed to study the question further. Under date of December 3, the minutes read: "Mrs. Druillard gave her report for a laundry as follows:"

VOTED, that we recommend that a room be built 14 x 16, sheeted and sided, with high windows, a partition to divide it crosswise; that the old stove be used for heating, and that a common boiler be provided for heating water." This plan was considered too small, and the committee was asked to reconsider the matter. After various changes, a larger building was provided for, and, in the minutes of Jan. 3, 1905, we read: "Prof. Sutherland reported 1400 feet of sheeting and 700 feet of siding on hand to build the laundry."

A building 30 feet square was finally put up, and Bro. Chas. Alden, then a member of the faculty, worked on the building. It is a plain frame building with a partition across the middle, the east end being finished for bath and toilet, a simple structure. This, with other buildings, was paid for from donations. It has served the school family eight years.

The laundry gradually became too small for both sanitarium and school purposes, and in the summer of 1912 a laundry building was erected near the sanitarium for the use of that institution and equipped with a gasoline mangle, the first bit of laundry machinery ever used on the place. A good many girls have paid their school expenses by work in the laundry. Three stationary tubs, wringers, an iron caldron for boiling, an ironing store, and ironing boards attached to the walls, will long be remembered as the primitive equipment for the laundry. Lady members of the faculty have taken their turns as matron of the department.

The school family has outgrown the bathroom facilities, and one of the next improvements will probably be the bath and laundry building for the school.

CHAPTER 13

BUILDINGS

According to the original plan submitted and adopted in October 1904, "Buildings are to be erected and equipped from gifts and donations." It was also noted that founders might put up cottages for themselves, with the understanding that should they desire to leave, the building would become the property of the school. Prof. Sutherland built a four-room cottage for his family in the northwest corner of the enclosure, then called the compound, a name given to the land within the stone wall which separated about three acres about Old Plantation from the rest of the farm. This was occupied in December 1904. Mrs. Druillard built a four-room cottage and occupied it in January 1905.

The building of laundry and bathrooms has been mentioned.

A two-room cottage was next built near the barns for the convenience of Bro. Brink and others who might have the care of the cattle. This was for some years known as Priscilla Cottage; whether because Bro. Brink fancied the name, or Bro. Alden had some family reasons for perpetuating the name, the records do not state. But it was later rechristened the Patton Cottage after the Patton family, who donated the price of the cottage.

The September 6, 1905 Union Meeting Minutes state that the committee on Cottage Building offered the following recommendation, which was adopted.

> That a two-room cottage be built on the campus east of Prof. Sutherland's cottage, 32 x 12 feet, with a back porch in style similar to Priscilla (Patton) Cottage, the foundation to be pillars instead of a wall, the walls to have sheeting and paper and to be plastered.

Prof. Sutherland had made his first trip through the West previous to this, and the Boulder (Colo.) Church donated the price for a cottage. This therefore became Boulder Cottage.

The mule and cow barn was a leaky old cedar log building standing directly in front of Old Plantation House and only about ten rods from that building, on the site now occupied by Catalan Hall, the present school building. About this time, it was decided to move the mules to the large barn where the cattle were kept, repair that building, and tear down the old cedar log barn, which was both unsightly and unsanitary. A donation from a lady interested in dairying made it possible to repair the cow barn, raising the roof building stanchions for the dairy herd, building a separator house, etc.

Tuesday, September 12, the minutes read:

> Build a cottage on the south side of the campus opposite Boulder Cottage, 28 x 32 feet, with four rooms, each with a closet, the closets to occupy the center of the house.

This became Nebraska Cottage, the gift of churches in the Nebraska Conference. This is the largest student cottage yet built, and has been occupied principally by lady students.

October 23, 1905, Mr. Alden, one of the founders, who had then been living one year on the $13.00 plan, "asked to be relieved of school duties while he painted Prof. Magan's cottage," as he wished to recuperate his finances, one way by which to live on $13 a month in a self-supporting school. About the same time other members of the faculty were granted the privilege of selling Christ's Object Lessons, which had been donated to the school, and which the school now turned over to these teachers to help them financially. That was another way to recruit the fading finances.

> November 20, 1905, "Voted, To build a room 12 x 14 near the laundry, in which cream and milk can be kept at proper temperature."

The cream house was certainly needed. It was built, just a simple plastered room containing a tank into which water was pumped from the well, the barrel chum, and other simple facilities. Later a storm cellar was put in at the back of this room, and the icebox, butter worker, etc., are kept there, and in summer the jars of cream and the molded butter are kept on ice.

The stones for this cellar were taken from the old stone wall, which had been built by slave labor and which enclosed the compound. This wall was torn away in front of Old Plantation, and the stone used in the foundations of Gotzian Hall.

Cottages and the stone fence at the Nashville Agricultural and Normal Institute, circa 1910.

CHAPTER 14

BREAD HOUSE

T he cooking for the school family was done in the kitchen of the Old Plantation House, and for a number of months the ordinary kitchen range did the family baking. As the family increased, however, this became an impossible task, and a one-room bake house, containing a Dutch oven, built of stone, was erected by Bro. Isaac Alcorn. This was located near the cream house, and stands about two rods back of the present dining hall. The Dutch oven did not prove entirely satisfactory. It was later torn down, and since then a galvanized iron oven, with a capacity of 60 loaves, was purchased. A little later a storeroom for flour and other supplies was built at the rear of the bread room. The work in the bakery has been carried by young women, usually by those who find it necessary to make their school expenses by work. Not a few have received their first lessons in bread making here under the tuition of Mrs. Druillard, Sister Mack, or Sister Ida Owen, who was a seamstress in Battle Creek and here. The building's being separated from others makes it possible to do the baking under the most advantageous conditions. The young woman who has charge of the baking is expected to keep the building in a neat, orderly condition, and many times visitors to the institution, when taken to that department, compliment the loaves of bread which come from the oven and the general appearance of the little room.

Up to the time that the Dixie Bakery began work, the school baked its own unleavened bread. This was especially true during the time that Sister Josephine Gotzian was connected with the institution. Zwiebach in quantities is provided for both the school and the sanitarium families.

In October 1905, the minutes of the Union Meeting show that the question of a dining hall was under consideration. There was a long discussion as to the proposed site. From that time on, various plans were drawn up for the building. Some felt that the old house should be used for dining purposes, and that it would be better to build a chapel. It seemed impossible to reach a decision in regard to a proper place to put up a dining hall, and finally on the last of October, it was voted that the rooms in the old house be used for kitchen and dining rooms without any alteration. It was then decided to put up a school building.

The means for this came in an interesting way. Prof. Sutherland was on the Pacific Coast. He had addressed an audience in Portland, telling them of the starting of the work in the South, and of Sister White's instruction that the work should be presented to our people, and that they should be given an opportunity to assist with their means. He was then asking for $25 donations. His faith had not yet risen above this sum. At the close of this particular meeting in Portland, a sister, Mrs. Phelps, who had heard his talk asked what she could do to assist this Southern movement. He told her of the $25 plan, which would make her a patron. She said, "I will become a patron: what else can I do?" For the first time, he suggested the idea of a school building. He told her of the need of a small school building, and gave her the approximate cost of a room 20 x 32. She said, "I will build it: what else can I do?" This of course seemed unusual and showed that the Lord had set his seal upon the work, and that, true to His promise, was touching the hearts of distant people to assist in this work. Phelps Hall, built just outside the line of the old stone wall, served for chapel and classroom purposes from the early part of 1906 until Gotzian Hall was completed in the fall of 1908. Since that time, it has been used for church school purposes a part of the time, and during the school year of 1911-12, when the attendance was large and the capacity of the cottages was insufficient, Phelps Hall was converted into a small dormitory for young women.

Bro. Chas. Sweeten of Ontario became interested in the building up of the institution, and spent a number of months in the school. One of his first works was the building of a small cottage east of Probation Hall. It is necessary to explain the meaning of the term, "Probation Hall." When the school first started, each young man was lodged in the original Negro quarters before referred to. It became a saying among them that that was a test of a student's persistence, and the term, "Probation Hall" was applied to

50

the building. One room in this building has now long been used as a cannery; another has been a storeroom for canned fruit; a third contains the carpenter's bench for repair work. But it is still known as Probation Hall.

The cottage just referred to was the second one erected for the young men. Priscilla or Patton Cottage came first; this second cottage was built on much the same plan, containing two rooms with an enclosed portion in the rear; it came as a result of a donation by the South Dakota Conference, and is known as the South Dakota Cottage.

Following this, three two-room cottages were built in the avenue laid out in the young men's section of the grounds. A new plan of building was carried out in the erection of these cottages. There were a number of young men on the place who desired to work at carpentry. Bro. Sweeten had charge of the work, and contracts were let to two young men at $75 each. This work was under the supervision of Bro. Sweeten. The cottages have since had ceilings installed on the inside and porches have been added. They are known respectively as the Oregon Cottage, the Upper Columbia Cottage, and Peach Cottage.

Practically all the building on the place has been done by students, under direction of our teachers in carpentry. Bro. Sweeten, Bro. Clement, Bro. Rocke, have acted as teachers. Buildings could he erected only when there was a fund on hand for building purposes, and only when there were students to do the work, and only when there was a demand for the room. These are the things which have guided in the speed with which the work has progressed.

Following the cottages already mentioned came Taylor Cottage, erected near the sanitarium, especially for the use of nurses, but much of the time used for patients when the rooms of the sanitarium proper were occupied. The twin cottages known as the Orin Miller and Mattheisen Cottages, named after their donors, and Davidson Cottage, standing on the edge of the groves northwest of the sanitarium, was first occupied by Sr. Lura Davidson, who donated it to the institution. This latter was occupied by Dr. Evans while he lived on the school farm. Later it was used by the sewing department, and the weaving industry was developed there.

The erection of the sanitarium, in 1907-1908, is a story by itself which will be treated afterwards.

CHAPTER 15

DINING HALL

One of the first buildings contemplated was a dining hall. When Sister White first wrote of the place, June 13, 1904, she said, "The farm has a roomy house, barns, and other buildings, and two and one-half miles of good stone fence."

This "roomy house," is said to be about 100 years old. The main part of it consisted of two log rooms, each about twenty feet square, connected by a hall. To the rear were built two other rooms, connected by a hallway. In this building, known as the Old Plantation House, practically every industry connected with the women's department had been carried on at some school room until Phelps Hall was built. The cooking was done in the family kitchen, and two of the rooms were used for dining purposes until the family became so large that it was almost impossible to walk between the tables. The rooms upstairs have been used for sleeping.

Practically all the early members of the faculty have lived in that building at some time. It was there that Prof. Alden and his wife lived the first year of their married life. It was there that Prof. Magan and his wife lived until their home was built. Prof. and Mrs. Sutherland graduated from Probation Hall into the Big Room, where they stayed till they built their house. Mother D. had her room upstairs, and Miss DeGraw as well; The office work was also done there for some years. The fireplace in this room would not draw unless the door was left open, so in winter time it was simply a question of freezing all the time or freezing on one side and roasting on the other.

Many and varied have been the plans suggested for remodeling the Plantation House. At times it was thought advisable to convert it into a school building, but the ceilings were low and the roofs in poor repair. At one time, it was thought to take out partitions and make one large dining room, but that was found to be impracticable. So nothing whatever was done to the old building, except to paint the outside and to patch the leaks in the roofs from time to time.

In the year 1911, definite plans were accepted for a new dining hall. After much discussion as to the proper location of the building, it was finally decided to erect it north of Old Plantation, some members of the faculty feeling that in time the Old Plantation House would be taken down.

The new dining hall, known as Kinne Hall in honor of the largest donor, became a dining room—34 x 42—a serving room, a kitchen, and a pantry. It is a story and a half high, the upper part being used for supplies. It was erected under the direction of Bro. Rocke, with Bro. A. L. Snyder having direct charge of the building force.

For eight years of the history of the institution, every bit of dishwater had been heated in a common boiler on the kitchen range. Kinne Hall is supplied with a hot-water tank, the water being piped into stationary sinks in the serving room and kitchen.

For eight years the family ate in the low, dark rooms in Old Plantation. There was general rejoicing when the whole family could assemble in the light, airy room of the new building. One of the comfortable features of this building is the large screened porch on the south side, where the workers in the department prepare vegetables, etc. Finished ceilings, painted a light green, cover the kitchen and serving room. The dining room has a plastered setting, and the side walls finished in burlap with a panel effect. Frequently visitors from the city have remarked upon the neat, artistic appearance of the building. It is one of the strongest arguments we can present in favor of the erection of buildings with student labor. It took nearly a year to put up the building, the young men working one-half day and carrying on their school work the other half. When farm work was pressing, the men of the building force would sometimes have to give up their work in order to help with the crops. Bad weather also sometimes hindered the work. Out of the whole experience, however, many valuable lessons were learned, lessons which have been impressed upon the workers in the institution under many and varied conditions. One of these lessons is that the fact that a building is needed does not always mean that that building will be forthcoming. First the money must be raised; then great pains must be taken if the work is to be done by students. Students who have had an actual part in the erection of such a building have a surpassing interest in the work of the institution. Students who have had a part in such work are qualified to meet the hardships and to do creative work in any field to which they are called.

In a leaflet entitled, *An Appeal for the Madison School*, Sister White says,

> The work at Madison not only educates for a knowledge of the Scriptures, but it gives a practical training that fits the student to go forth as a self-supporting missionary to the fields to which he is called. . . . The students have been taught to raise their own crops, to build their own houses, and to care wisely for cattle and poultry. They have been learning to become self-supporting, and a training more important than this they cannot receive. Thus they have obtained a valuable education for usefulness in missionary fields.

Kinne Hall stands as a memorial to this kind of work.

Edward and Sallie (Bralliar) Sutherland,
Photograph taken 1897 in Battle Creek, Michigan.

CHAPTER 16

GOTZIAN HALL

The story of Gotzian Hall reads like some fairy tale, and contains lessons by which some of us may profit. We little know, when we are passing through certain experiences, how the influence of our lives will be woven into future events.

Some twenty-five years ago a young man was sent out from Battle Creek College to canvass during the vacation. He went into the Minnesota Conference and was assigned a place in the home of a well-to-do Sabbath-keeper who was a widow. Other young men had lived in this family, but because they could not go and come as they pleased or could not have exactly the kind of food they wanted to eat, they really found life unpleasant there. This young man made up his mind he would please this sister if it was possible. He groomed her horse and did other work about the place for his board and room. The sister looked with favor on the young canvasser, and afterwards kept a warm place in her heart for him.

During one of his trips to the Pacific Coast, Professor Sutherland had the privilege of presenting the needs of this work in California. Among others whom he visited was his old-time friend, Sister Josephine Gotzian, formerly of Minnesota. When he talked of the needs of the South, Sister Gotzian responded with a gift of $100. Little more was said about it at the time, but later Sister Gotzian made a trip south, and spent about a year with the school family of the Nashville Agricultural and Normal Institute. To Sister Gotzian we are indebted for our present school building, known as Gotzian Hall. Gotzian Hall stands on the south side of the road that approaches Old Plantation, and just west of the old stone wall which formed the boundary of the old compound. Two massive stone pillars originally guarded the entrance. Their large flat stones went into the foundation of Gotzian Hall. Bro. W. G. Clement, of College View, Nebraska was the architect.

The building occupies almost the exact site of the old mule barn. Gotzian Hall is a plain building, with a floor space of about 2250 feet. It has but one story and contains an assembly room with a seating capacity of 250. The rear part of this room is separated by folding doors, and makes two large recitation rooms. The Marian Davis reading room occupies the southwest corner of the building, and the president's office a small room on the northwest. The building can be entered from the north and from the east. It is a commodious, plain structure, and has proven decidedly satisfactory as a school building. It is well-lit and airy. It is furnished with arm-chairs, a piano, and a rostrum on which is the speaker's desk. It is used for school and church purposes, since the Madison Church Organization has no building of its own. It is thoroughly screened, and class-work is carried on throughout the summer with comparative comfort. It cost between $2500 and $3000.

From the platform in Gotzian Hall have been delivered notable addresses, and that assembly room, small as it is, has witnessed some intensely interesting meetings.

The building was dedicated in October 1908 at the first annual convention of self-supporting workers. This meeting brought together about 150 people. In April 1909, Sister White visited the institution for the first time after the purchase of the property. In addressing the students, she gave that instruction now printed in pamphlet form, and entitled, *Words of Encouragement for Self-supporting Workers*. It was on this occasion that she used, probably for the first time, the term, "hill schools."

After describing the purchase of the property, in which she had had a part, she said:

> For a time the prospect looked forbidding. Nevertheless, the plantation
> was secured and the work was begun. The Lord would have the influence
> of this school widely extended by means of the establishment of small
> mission schools in needy settlements in the hills, where consecrated
> teachers may open the Scriptures to hungry souls and let the light of life
> shine forth to those that are in darkness. This is the very work that
> Christ did. ... As you engage in schoolwork in these needy communities,

do not let any man come in to discourage you by saying, 'Why do you spend your time in this way? Why not do a larger and more important work in a broader field?' . . .We feel an earnest interest in these schools. There is a wide field before us in the establishment of family mission schools. . . We are glad, very glad, for the evidences of prosperity attending the work here at Madison. To everyone assembled at this Institute, I would say, 'Search the Scriptures. If you do not fully realize the times in which you live and the nearness of the end, seek to gain a fuller realization of these things by searching the Scriptures. There is a work to be done in every place. We must seek to catch the very spirit of the message.

The significance of these words, addressed to the little company of workers who were at that time struggling with the problems of self-support in various little school centers, will be recognized by all. Those who read these words can understand how full of encouragement were such expressions as these:

When I first visited Madison about five years ago and looked over this school property, I told those who were with me, that in appearance it was similar to one of the places that had been presented before me in vision during the night season—a place where our people would have opportunity of presenting the light of truth to those who had never heard the last gospel message. ...

I am glad that our people are established here at Madison. I am glad to meet these workers here, who are offering themselves to go to different places. God s work is to advance steadily; His truth is to triumph. To every believer we would say: 'Say not, "We cannot afford to work in a sparsely-settled field, and largely in a self-supporting way, when out in the world are great fields where we might reach multitudes." And let none say, 'We cannot afford to sustain you in an effort to work in those out-of-the-way places.' What! Cannot afford it! You cannot afford not to work in these isolated places; and if you neglect such fields, the time will come when you will wish that you had afforded it.

Since that time, four other similar meetings have been held in Gotzian Hall. These are the annual conventions of self-supporting workers. Each year more workers of this character have been brought together. These meetings have varied from time to time, and have brought into our midst men who are deeply interested in this movement, for various reasons. Among speakers who have addressed the student body from the rostrum in Gotzian Hall are a number of instructors from the agricultural college of the University of Tennessee: Prof. H. A. Morgan, Prof. Chas. A Keiffer, Prof. Barnes, and others who have given instruction to our student body because they are in harmony with the effort being made by this institution to elevate agriculture as an industry. Hon. John Thompson, the head of the agricultural work of the state, spoke in most encouraging terms of the work we are attempting to do. Prof. Anderson, County Superintendent of Education, gave a most interesting educational talk. Miss Virginia Moore, State Director of the School Improvement Association; Miss Mary Hannah Johnson, the former active librarian of Nashville; Mrs. L. H. Harris, a well-known southern author; Prof. Mack A. Miller, formerly of Ruskin College, Chicago, who with his company of workers is developing an industrial institution in Florida.

One of the most thrilling talks on education was given by Dr. P. P. Claxton, United States Commissioner of Education, in April 1912. Dr. Claxton had become acquainted with the work of the Madison School through friends who had been patients at the Rural Sanitarium. In addressing the student body, he uttered some principles so applicable to the work being done here that if he had studied the work of the school firsthand and the Spirit of Prophecy, he could scarcely have handled the subject in a more appropriate way.

Among those who have given religious instruction or who have carried a burden for our own denominational work are Elder Daniells, who has visited the place twice; Prof. Frederick Griggs, who was here in the early history of this institution; Prof. H. R. Salisbury, Educational Superintendent, whose last visit was in the winter of 1912; Elder S. M. Haskell and Sister Haskell. Elder Haskell has from the beginning of our work been the president of our Board of Managers, and is looked upon in the nature of a father to the institution. Always when he is here, we esteem it a privilege to sit at his feet as Bible student(s).

Elder Geo. I. Butler was one of our earliest staunch friends.

Elder. W. H. Anderson, on his return trip to Central Africa, addressed our students regarding self-supporting educational work in the Dark Continent. Elder McVagh, Union Conference President, so long as he remained in the South, was a frequent visitor. Elder C. P. Bollman, Elder W. H. Burrows, Elder. B. W. Brown of Kentucky, who has made a number of earnest pleas for workers for his state. Elder Albert Prieger of Alabama has done the same for his state. Elder Geo. M. Brown of North Carolina has always shown his interest in our work.

But some of the most interesting educational stories the walls of this assembly room might tell if given the power of utterance are the pleas made in self-defence by some members of the Union Body under discipline, or the debates, clear, fresh, and up-to-date, made for some items of work that specially touched the student's heart. Whether it be the placid countenance of the president of the institution, as he guides the assembly through some turbulent meeting, or the good-natured face of the Irish dean as he makes a characteristic speech, these rooms see and hear some interesting things.

Gotzian Hall.
Photo taken sometime after this manuscript was written.

CHAPTER 17

DRUMMING UP SUPPORT

By Percy T. Magan

I went to a camp meeting or two in the North (1904), and I did not figure on the thing anymore for awhile. I [then] went home to Ireland, as you know. I came back in January. All I did the next year was to work on the farm. My health was wretched. We prayed a good deal for money for a schoolroom, but didn't get any. We held school in the old house that summer Mrs. Sutherland was up north. I never went out on a money trip till February 1906. Sutherland had gotten all the money we had had. He did a lot of work in Battle Creek, and was quite successful there in getting small pledges. Then he went west and got some good pledges, the beginning of our building fund. And Sutherland had gotten more money altogether for this thing than I had.

I went east, and Sands Lane, who was then president of the New York Conference, was there to welcome me. There was an old lady in that state whom I had never met; she was not an Adventist, but she had sent us money at Berrien. This old lady I went to see.

I went to the house, a magnificent mansion, and sent in my card. By and by one of the most beautiful-looking old ladies I ever saw came in: a dignified, handsome, religious-looking woman. She stretched out both her hands to me, took my hand between her two, and told me how she had often wanted to meet me, had always enjoyed my letters, how I had never begged for money, but had just told her of conditions and opportunities. I sat and chatted with her all the afternoon. I told her I must go on that evening. I did not ask her for any money, but she said she was going to help us in our new work in the South. She wanted me to pray for her brother, who was very ill. We had a season of prayer that night. I told her I was going on to Boston. She wanted me to take a sleeper, but I told her No. She asked, "Because you cannot afford it?" "Yes." She said, "I will pay for it." I thanked her, but refused; she was that tender and solicitous all the time.

I left that night and went to Boston. Charlie Nicola was there; he was a bit of a heretic himself, and he was kind to me. Elder Place was there; he was president of the Conference; told me I might get anything I could. I got small sums there, $35 from this and $25 from that, etc. But I made friends with some very fine people in Boston, and all of that. I went then to New Bedford and picked up quite a few pledges there, probably three or four hundred dollars. It was pretty small picking, but it was the only thing in sight; all the rest of the country was closed to us. Then Melrose helped me quite a lot, the nurses and Nicola and his wife. Then I had some experiences. I was invited to speak at the Y.W.C.A. in Boston. I met B. O. Flower, editor of the Arena; he put a notice in the Arena about our work. I had some experiences that cheered me up a bit, and then I went back to New York and joined Sands Lane. He told me I might go around with him to the churches. He thought I would probably get $25 or so in each church. We were trying to make up a dairy: five cows would keep a student in school; cowships in place of scholarships—our dairy has been our main work.

The picking was hard. I went down to Watertown, N. Y., to Isadora Green She was a dear old friend. I had a nice time with her. She was struggling herself to establish her work there. I did not ask her for any money. While there I got a letter from Will White in which he told me of how Daniells accused me of being at best the hind leg of the devil in the old benevolence business.

I thought I would take no stock in it, but he demanded that I go to Washington and explain things. I think my wife had read the letter to the folks here, and they thought I had better go on. I was not keen to go, but I prayed over the matter and counselled with Isadora Green. She was very nice, and said, "I'll stand by you folks. I don't believe any of this trash, and I'll help you what little I can at Washington, for I did not know how I was going to get through with that thing."

They were feeling mean and ugly, and would not believe what we told them. When I got up from my knees that night, I knew that something had happened somewhere, and that God had heard the poor prayers I was offering, and that I would get through that experience all right, and it was not the only experience I would have. I was just as light-hearted as I could be.

I did not feel like hurrying down there. I went over to New Jersey to Summit Heights, a very swell place. In some way I had received word that this Mrs.___ , who sent us that $800, was there. She was a woman whom I had brought into the truth in Battle Creek in years past, a woman who built the church for them in _____. She always felt very friendly toward me. I went to the post office and asked if there was a Mrs. ____ there. They said it was against the law to tell. I felt like not giving up, and I went over to a drugstore and asked the drugstore man. He said, "Yes! How did you ever dream of coming to me to ask about her?" I said, "I don't know; I just came." He said, "She's out at the Milk Sanitarium, about three miles out in the country." So I started out afoot to the Milk Sanitarium. It was a lovely April morning. I went out and rang the bell. A servant came to the door, and I asked for her.

I proved myself a proper person to be admitted, and then they let me in to see her. She was very glad to see me. I sat and chatted with her, telling her all about our work. She was in great trouble of mind. She did not care two cents for her husband; he was one of the best men who ever lived, and she was having a struggle about getting a divorce from him. I think afterwards she did go off with a man and is living with him now, if she is not dead. She unburdened her heart to me, and I tried to advise her in a good way. She had not lived with her husband for years.

I did not ask her for any money, but when she bade me goodbye, she said, "Now I'll not forget you, for the Lord has impressed me more than once to help you." That milk cure she was trying put the idea into her head, I suppose, to help us in the dairy, and she gave $500 to put up a barn. I left her then with no special promise of any money, but I felt pretty sure I would get it. I was afterwards up in Minnesota, and had asked permission of the conference committee to go through their churches, and had been turned down by that man Shaw. The minute after I had been turned down, a letter was put into my hand, telling how she had sent this $800.

I left Summit Heights that morning, and took the morning train. That night I took the train that night for Washington. When I got there, the brethren would hardly speak to me. I never had gotten such a cold shoulder in all my days before. No man asked me where I dwelt or how I fared. So I went to my old enemies the Hairds, and they asked me to come in. They were feeling very badly, for they had quarreled with the brethren. The Missus cried and said she was sorry she had said so many mean things; and I forgave her, and we lived happily ever after. Butler was there, and I knew the old man would be my friend as far as he dared. I went to him and said, "Now I am here because Will White told me to come, but I'm never going to ask to come into this council, though I have worked for the General Conference twenty years. If they want me in, they may invite me; if not, I'll go home. You act as my ambassador now." So he said he would, and he went to Daniells. Daniells said he didn't know; he didn't feel very free to have Bro. Magan come in. The old man came and reported to me. I said, "All right! I'll take the night train. I don't care to row with those fellows."

Before I had time to take the train, however, they had decided I was to come in. They were holding the meeting in the room which I call the Four-and-Twenty Elders, with its big revolving chairs ail screwed down to the floor. They were having their meeting there. I sat in a corner; I was not asked to take any place among them. I knew I was a black sheep in the midst of God's children; so I sat and sucked my thumb and listened. In the course of things, Farnsworth got up and he blew along at a great rate, how he didn't think anything should be on a private basis. He jumped around like a hen with her head off on a hot johnnycake.

I knew they were all thinking of getting a speech from me. They passed a law in substance resolving that no person or persons or any corporation not under the direct control or ownership of this or local conference should have any right to go out and solicit help. I sat in my corner and wagged my foot; and I thought, "Now you've passed that thing; the next thing will be to enforce it." But I said nothing. There was an awkward silence. They asked me if I had anything to say. I said, "No." I was not going to tell them I was going out to break their law.

They took a recess then, and I went out. They had a bathroom-like place in the back of the hall, where they washed their hands. I went in there, and stood there with my back to four or five of them, my face to the window. I felt pretty sober; the outlook was blue. Ed felt he had done all he could in California; things were closing like this here; and I felt like Noah's dove, no place to rest my foot. And we still needed a whole lot. I had not been getting money fast. Sands Lane was about the only fellow who would let me into his bailiwick.

Then someone came up behind me and put his arm around my shoulder, and a good-natured, gruff voice said, "My boy, don't you feel bad about this. These fellows have gone wild, and I don't take any stock in it. When you fellows get so you can't wiggle, you come up to my country, and I'll help you." It was old Brother Underwood; his eyes were full of tears. That was the beginning of our northwestern business. It came as the result of their fandango there in Washington. I never dreamed Underwood would befriend me; he had trained with the stand-pat class of chaps; but he lined up straight from that time on.

Then I had a meeting with Daniells and Butler, and they wanted to know about this, that, and the other. I saw they didn't understand things at all. One thing against me (and that involved all of us) was that I had been present at a meeting in Battle Creek where they had voted two or three things. One thing, I had made a motion in a meeting of a concern we had to hold the old Battle Creek College property, to give a quit-claim deed for $1 of the ground on which the fire station stood, to the B. C. San., and they had construed that as meaning that I was just ruthlessly handing away valuable denominational property to the sanitarium. The fact established the paid by collections from citizens about there, but while the city held title, the deed read that it should revert to the college when it should cease to be a fire station property; and now they proposed to give the West End a bigger and better station if we would release this property to the Sanitarium, which was giving her fire apparatus and other concessions to the city. Another thing was that at a meeting of the Benevolent Association when I was present, they had voted to turn over to the Sanitarium a house and lot they owned in Battle Creek. Another was I had sanctioned the move whereby they got hold of Guadalajara. Another, that I had made a motion to adjourn to meet at Berrien Springs, where everyone had resigned.

Just at the close of the conference, Daniells came to me, and he said, "I suppose you have had a copy of this."

I said, "No, I have not had any mail since I have been here. He handed me a document. It was from Sister White to that whole General Conference Council. We were standing on the steps of their new General Conference Building. He says, Now I want to accept that and believe it, and you go and read it, and I will talk with you later." I went down around the building and read it.

April 4: I looked at the date of it, and it was that same day I had been on my knees in New York City. I had not written to Sister White about matters; I had not written her for about a year, and certainly had not written her one word about this thing; but that testimony bore that same identical date. I knew it had meant something when I was in New York that time.

CHAPTER 18

THE WATER PLANT

When the property was purchased for the Madison School, there was on the place one well, located near Old Plantation House. Over this well stood a windmill, and on the north side of Old Plantation stood two tanks, into which the water could be pumped. This supplied water to the kitchen. A cistern was located a few feet east of the building. This was the water supply on the farm. During the late summer and autumn of each year the water in the well ran so low that it was almost impossible to supply the needs of the family. Each year it was a great question how to get the water for the cattle. During the dry season Bro. Brink would drive the cows to the river, but the bank of the river was dangerously steep, and the cattle would suffer thirst rather than go down to the water.

For a time, an effort was made to pump water by hand from the river for the cattle. Later, three drilled wells were put in, in an attempt to get a supply of water sufficient for the stock and the school family. A sanitarium was contemplated, and an abundant supply of water was needed there.

In no case was it found possible to secure a strong enough stream of water to ensure a supply during the entire year. The problem became a perplexing one. Bro. Gotfredson, Elder Daniells, Elder W. C. White, and others looked over the situation and advised putting in a water plant that would meet the needs of the institution. Bro. Joseph Sutherland, for years business manager at Union College, gave the experience of that institution in securing a water supply, and it was his suggestion that with the Cumberland River so near, a pumping plant should be installed that would enable us to utilize river water. There was some talk of building large cisterns, of putting in above-ground tanks, and other schemes. It was finally decided to put a pumping plant on the riverbank, pipe the water to the highest place on the grounds, locate a tank there, and from there pipe it to

the barns, the sanitarium, the school bathrooms, and the dining department.

Professor Magan superintended the work, and Bro. Geo. Hill of Mil-
waukee had the oversight of the actual work. A 43,000-gallon cypress tank
was placed on a 30-foot pine tower, and a 10-horsepower gasoline engine
was located in a small pumping house on the riverbank, on the tract known
as the hundred-acres, lying on the south side of the Neely's Bend Road.
The pump will force 90 gallons a minute through the 3,655 feet of pipe,
with 250-feet vertical lift. The cost of the plant was about $5,000. This
plant has proved decidedly satisfactory, making it possible to continue the
work of the dairy and carry on the work of the sanitarium.

CHAPTER 19

THE SANITARIUM

When Sister White visited the Ferguson Farm before it was purchased for a school, she spent a number of hours on the place in company with Elder W. C. White, Elder J. E. White, Bro. W. O. Palmer, Mrs. Druillard, Professor Magan, and others; and the company ate lunch under the trees in a little clearing on the place, not far from where Mrs. Druillard's cottage now stands. As they sat there, Sister White looked around and said, "This would be a good location for your sanitarium."

From that time on, she seemed never to lose sight of the fact that the Madison School should have connected with it a sanitarium. Concerning this, she writes, "Early in the history of the Madison School it was suggested that a sanitarium might be established on a portion of the property purchased for the school farm." In letters written to those in charge of the medical missionary work in the southern states, and pointing out the advantages that are gained by establishing a training school and a sanitarium in close proximity, in the fall of 1904, she says,

> One institution will give influence and strength to the other; and, too, money can be saved by both institutions, because each can share the advantages of the other.

Again she wrote, after speaking of the work to be done in the Madison School in training students to be self-supporting:

> To this is added the knowledge of how to treat the sick and to care for the injured. This training for medical missionary work is one of the grandest objects for which any school can be established. . . . It is essential that there shall be a sanitarium connected with the Madison school.

The educational work at the school and the sanitarium can go forward hand in hand. The instruction given at the school will benefit the patients, and the instruction given to the sanitarium patients will be a blessing to the school.

For the first year or more, it seemed that the energy of the workers was exhausted in the building up of the farm. However, the thought of the sanitarium was never lost.

In the spring of 1906, Dr. O. M. Hayward and Bro. L. A. Hansen, sanitarium workers in the city of Nashville, began to search for a suitable site on which to locate a country sanitarium. Dr. Hayward had been doing work in the city for several years, and was well known among prominent people of the city. He had rented a small place in the suburbs, to which he sent patients needing country air and quiet, but it was felt that property should be purchased and suitable buildings erected. They looked at various places about the city, having their attention directed to the Boscobel property and others. Sister White advised the brethren to consider carefully the locating of a sanitarium on the Madison School farm. The brethren felt that when the school was located, the needs of a sanitarium had not been considered and that the Madison School property was too far from the city of Nashville, and they advised the Madison management to sell this place and purchase the Sanford property on Dickerson Pike, with the idea of connecting school and sanitarium.

Bro. Baldwin, of Oklahoma, visited Nashville, with the idea of assisting in the erection of the Nashville Sanitarium. Several communications passed between Sister White and those who were in search of a place. She urged them to locate on the Madison Farm, stating that it was not too far from Nashville and that it was a favorable location for a sanitarium. Bro. Baldwin and Dr. J. B. Caldwell, who was then connected with the Nashville Sanitarium work, visited the Madison School Farm. At one time the school offered the Sanitarium workers 100 acres of the best land on the place for sanitarium purposes. But it was decided that this was too far away from Nashville. The Southern Union Conference therefore decided to locate a sanitarium of their own near the city and to encourage the school to build a small Rural Sanitarium on their own property.

In the summer of 1905, before any steps had been taken toward building a sanitarium, there came to the Madison School a man whose home was in the city of Nashville. He was suffering from disease and wanted a quiet place in which to recuperate. He stated that he had heard something of the Battle Creek system of treatments and the dietary advocated by the Battle Creek Sanitarium. He thought he could receive the treatments here, but the Madison School was in no position whatever to care for sick people. He begged, however, to stay, and he was given the privilege of sleeping on the veranda of the old house. He was supplied with food from the students' table, not because we were soliciting a patient, but because he insisted on staying. Gradually the man's strength returned to him. He returned to his home in Nashville and resumed his business. To his friends he gave the credit of his recovery to the healthful diet, the quiet surroundings, and the cheerful atmosphere of the school farm.

It would seem that God endeavored to impress upon our minds at that time, when the idea of a sanitarium seemed almost too large for us, to undertake, that He wanted the sick to be healed here. Sister White wrote to Sister Druillard about the work of the school, telling her that, like Esther of old, it was her privilege to unite with this institution and to help it with her means. She added that if Sister Druillard did not see light in that, God would raise up someone else. Like Esther, she responded to the call, and no one connected with the institution has had more to do in shaping the policy of the Rural Sanitarium than Sister Druillard.

In June 1906, a meeting was held in Phelps Hall to consider plans for the present. Bro. J. E. White also attended the meeting. At that time Bro. Pflugradt promised $5,000 toward the sanitarium enterprise. While this money never came into the institution, it was not long till others became interested in it, and arrangements were made to begin building.

Sister Josephine Gotzian, whose life has been devoted largely to sanitarium work, put $3,000 into this enterprise. Sister E. C. Grey, Sr. Phelps, and Bro. Nis Hansen all gave liberally to the sanitarium fund. Many people helped with smaller sums. Sister White, writing to the workers at Madison, says, "I am instructed to say to those who have means to spare, 'Help the work at Madison. You have no time to lose. Satan will soon rise up to create hindrances. Let the work go forward while it may.'" Men and women of means, hearing the call for help, responded liberally.

The Cumberland River Near Madison College

CHAPTER 20

THE SANITARIUM LOCATION

For some time it was a question just where to locate the sanitarium. Sister White had said, "I have been instructed that there are decided advantages to be gained by the establishment of a school and a sanitarium in close proximity." On the 100-acre tract there is a high hill overlooking the Cumberland River, and by some this was considered an ideal spot for the sanitarium. Others felt that it would be wiser to locate the buildings in the locust grove near the Neelys Bend Road, opposite the hundred acres.

It was finally decided to put the buildings near that part of the farm where Sister White was sitting when she ate her picnic lunch in June 1904 and said to the company, "This is a favorable site for your sanitarium."

It was the purpose of the managers of the institution to build the sanitarium, not as a distinct institution, but as an integral part of the school. Certain well-defined principles were being worked out in other parts of the institution: there was a reason for building cottages for students instead of putting up one large dormitory. If the sanitarium should become a part of the school, the same general plan of building should be followed, but nowhere was such a sanitarium to be found; no other institution seemed to have passed over this same experience, and the way had to be blazed for this without a precedent. Many were the studies instituted concerning God's plan for sanitarium work.

Almost from the beginning of our denomination, He has given to us the principles of diet reform, the benefits of simple life in close touch with nature, the value of water, fresh air, sunshine, and properly directed exercise, in the cure of disease. The whole plan of the school was in harmony with the call back to the country, and in harmony with this same call it was decided to erect a one-story building for a sanitarium. Plans were drawn and redrawn. New light would come in as the subject was studied. At last the patient rooms were built together in the form of an L, each room an outside room on the ground floor, thoroughly ventilated, well-lit, opening upon a broad veranda. Ten feet from the limb of the L, the bathrooms were located. These are in a square building one story in height. The building contains gentlemen's and ladies' bath and treatment rooms and physicians' offices. The veranda continues from the patients rooms across the front of the bathrooms. In front of the bathrooms, and leaving an open court about 50 feet square, stands the dining hall. This building contains the parlor, dining room, kitchen, and an office, and is connected with the other portions of the building by a covered way. This means that there is a continuous covered way from the patient rooms to the bathrooms and the dining room, making it possible for patients to spend a large amount of time outdoors in any kind of weather. This is one of the unique features of the institution. In fact, it becomes the living quarters for many of the patients twenty-four hours a day.

Mrs. Druillard, Dr. Lillian Magan, Prof. Sutherland, Prof. Magan, and others are responsible for the general plan of the building, and while some changes would probably be made were the building to be done over, the general plan has proved decidedly satisfactory. To most people the name "sanitarium" conveys the idea of an immense building, with elevators, steam heat, expensive apparatus, gymnasium equipped with many artificial appliances for exercise, and an atmosphere of artificial life. When one enters the Madison Rural Sanitarium, the contrast is so strong it frequently calls forth an exclamation of wonder.

The building is surrounded by trees. The view in every direction is beautiful, and the quiet is impressive. Patients accustomed to the noise and the smoke-laden air of the city, at once appreciate the quiet of the Rural Sanitarium.

For a time Dr. Lillian Magan was the only physician. Later, Dr. Newton Evans moved his family to the school farm, and while teaching in one of the medical schools in Nashville, acted for two years as superintendent of the Rural Sanitarium. The services of Dr. Evans as superintendent continued even after he left Nashville, and both he and Dr. W. H. Mason showed their faith in this work, and manifested their interest in its success, by retaining their places on the medical staff. Dr. Emma Laird rendered valuable assistance as house physician and as teacher in the nurses' classes from October 1911 until March 1912, when she and Elder Laird left Madison to start a work of their own.

In January 1908, as the building was nearing completion, Dr. R. M. Martinson offered to install the bathroom appliances. The equipment of the sanitarium is decidedly simple. It is the purpose to utilize to the fullest extent the rational remedies suggested by the Spirit of Prophecy. The furnishings of the sanitarium are simple, but the rooms are neat and comfortable.

The institution was dedicated in June 1908, as soon as the completion of the water plant made it possible to secure a supply of water in the building. Mrs. Sutherland was first chosen as the superintendent of the new department of the institution. Later Mrs. Piper acted as matron, but during the greater part of the history of the institution, Mrs. Druillard has been the familiar figure and the moving spirit in the work. It is she who meets the patients, looks after their wants, guides the work of the nurses and student helpers. No appropriate title has been found to designate the one who carries such a multitude of burdens; she is known to patients and students alike as "Mother D."

The no-debt policy was adopted when the Madison School farm was purchased, and that policy has been strictly adhered to during the life of the institution. The sanitarium patronage began with just a few patients. It had to build up a reputation. People would often say, "I never knew there was such an institution as this within reach of Nashville. Why don't you advertise?" And the answer was, "We build slowly. Well-pleased patients are our best advertisements." And so it has proved. Quietly and gradually our patronage has been built up. Influential people in Nashville have found that within easy reach of their own homes there is a quiet little retreat where rational treatments are given, and where patients are well-cared-for. The no-debt policy has been carried out, not because of the large number of patients handled, nor because of high rates charged, but because of strict economy practiced in every detail of the management. With the school and the sanitarium in close proximity, it is possible for the sanitarium to be run without a large corps of paid workers. When the patronage is low, the nurses and helpers find work in other parts of the institution. When the patronage is high, the school itself bends every energy and sacrifices as

77

it may be necessary to furnish the extra help needed at the sanitarium. The patronage has steadily increased, until at times there are a number of patients waiting an opportunity to be received. The capacity of the institution is usually considered to be fifteen. By crowding and by utilizing cottage room, twenty-five have at times been accommodated.

Madison College class of 1914.
Photo was taken two years after this manuscript was written.

CHAPTER 21

DONATIONS

The list of donors to the Nashville Agricultural and Normal School and its auxiliary schools will constitute a roll of honor worthy of publication. Early in the history of the school, Sister White wrote concerning giving as follows:

> Every possible means should be devised to establish schools of the Madison order in various parts of the South, and those who lend their means and their influence to this work are aiding the cause of God. I am instructed to say to those who have means to spare, 'Help the work at Madison. You have no time to lose. Satan will soon rise up to create hindrances. Let the work go forward while it may'. . . . Brethren Sutherland and Magan should be encouraged to solicit means for the support of their work. It is the privilege of these brethren to receive gifts from any of the people whom God impresses to help. They should have means, God's means, with which to work. The Madison enterprise has been crippled in the past, but now it must go forward.

The first intention of those who established this school was to bear the financial burden entirely alone. They had no idea of asking financial help from anyone else. They realized that it was apt to bring friction. But the instruction given by Sister White was clear and convincing on this point; Paul wrote to the Philippian church that he asked donations of them for his self-supporting work, not alone because it helped his work, but because the giving proved a blessing to the donor. He says, "In Thessalonica ye sent once and again unto my necessity, not because I desire a gift, but I desire fruit that may abound to your account," Phil. 4:16,17.

The workers in the Nashville Agricultural and Normal Institute could not ask for kinder or more liberal friends. They have felt free to ask donations for the same reason that Paul did. Frequently the donation of money has been the first step taken by the donor toward getting into the South himself. It is first the money, then the man. Donations have been of various sizes, and have come in various forms. Every building on the place, with the exception of teachers' cottages, which they themselves paid for, every building, the water plant, the sanitarium, the new road, and equipment in various forms, have come as the result of donations, usually given for some specific purpose.

Even before the company came to the South, interested friends had begun to donate toward the new enterprise. A large number of students at Berrien Springs sold Christ's Object Lessons for the benefit of the work. As a part of the original plan in building up the work at Madison, each person who gave $25 or more was made a shareholder or patron of the institution, which entitled him to one vote in the annual meeting of the Board of Managers. The patrons of the Nashville Agricultural and Normal Institute are scattered from the Atlantic to the Pacific. Many in this way have a living interest in the cause which the Madison School represents.

The story of buildings and equipment is the story of donations. There have been, however, many other donations made to the school. In November 1905, Prof. Floyd Bralliar, principal of Stuart Academy, Iowa, donated 1,000 strawberry plants. This was the beginning of fruit raising on the farm. That same fall, furniture was needed for student rooms, and money for this was solicited by Mrs. Druillard and Miss DeGraw. Students have sometimes been tempted to complain over the meager furniture, but they are always told that the school management will buy furniture whenever there is money in the furniture fund, but we go without when we have no money. The price of the kitchen range was raised by ladies in the College View (Neb.) church. In the summer of 1911, a new milk wagon was needed for marketing, and Bro. and Sr. Schee donated the price of the wagon.

During the first years of the Institute, there was practically no fruit raised on the farm. The school was poor; very little cash was raised, because most of the students paid their way by working, and the diet was confined to a few staple articles. At that time Sister White sent from her farm in California a donation of dried fruit. Those who have lived under similar conditions can imagine the hearty appreciation with which this gift was received. Twice, a large shipment of fruit has come from California friends, largely through the solicitation of Sr. E. C. Grey. Part of this has been used by the Madison School, and the rest has been distributed among the Highland School and the various colored schools in the South.

Through the kindness of Bro. W. K. Kellogg, the school has received large donations of corn flakes and toasted wheat flakes. At various times friends have donated the price of one or more cows, because the dairy herd made work for young men, who thus met their school expenses. Money has been donated for horses, also. Church school children have donated the quilts they pieced in their classes to this and other schools. They have sold papers to make money to buy fruit trees for the school orchard. In fact, the orchard on the Madison School farm was started by a ten-cent-a-tree campaign.

Young People's Societies have studied the South through the aid of teachers or students, and have sometimes donated to help struggling highland schools, sometimes to help students who needed cash in their school work, or for the loom recently purchased for the weaving of rugs. Members of the Lodi Sabbath School donated the money to furnish a room at the sanitarium. When it became necessary to have some better system of lighting the sanitarium than kerosene lamps, donations were solicited for an acetylene lighting plant.

Many lessons have been learned during the growing years of this institution. When a work is built up in this way, people must learn that they do not always get what they think they need at exactly the time they think they need it. They learn to consider well before they ask for help, and they learn to wait patiently for the Lord's Spirit to impress hearts with what they should give.

In one of his trips West, Prof. Sutherland heard of a man who owned a large ranch. One stormy night, he reached a station seven miles from the ranch just about dusk. He had an appointment several miles away for the next day, so he had but a few hours for this place. With a livery rig he drove out to the ranch. He had never seen the owner before, but the owner had already heard something of the work in the South and the starting of the Madison School. The interview began about nine o'clock in the evening. The story of the move to the South and other plans for the work here were told. Some of the needs were presented. The ranchman and his wife listened with attention for an hour and a half, and there were indications that they were much affected by the story. As he left the home near midnight in order to catch an early morning train, the man and his wife, after a brief council, gave him a donation of $500. This was his second experience in receiving gifts of any considerable size. He was learning to tell the story without asking for any definite donations, and to trust to the Spirit of God to put it into the hearts of men to give. On the way to the station, he was lost in a 1200-acre wheat field, but present inconveniences were lightly esteemed in view of the fact that God was rewarding his efforts.

It was some such experiences as this that gave courage to present the needs of the work under trying circumstances. In the year 1905, he spent two days in the home of a lady who was known to have helped various enterprises in a generous way. He told her the story of the work in the South. He did not ask her for money, but on leaving she promised help later. She investigated the work at Madison, and after a few months a check for $50 was received, with a promise to give more later on. Previous experiences had led to manifest evidences that Gad knew when money was needed, and that it was unnecessary to worry because a donation seemed small. Three years later, when there was a pressing need for help in building the sanitarium and for making other improvements, this same person gave at one time $2,000, and a few weeks later another $1,000. That first visit, while it seemed to yield a very small crop, evidently saw some seed planted, and the fruit was garnered later. Such experiences teach one to have faith in God.

This experience of waiting is not confined to finances. The school has often had the same experience in dealing with people. One of the most ardent workers in the South at the present time was formerly a county superintendent in Pennsylvania. For three years in succession an earnest effort was made to get him into the church school work, but he was too much absorbed in the public schools to give any serious thought to denominational work. At last, however, as the result of persistent effort, he attended a summer school at Berrien Springs. Instead of returning to his work in the fall, he resigned his position, remained at Berrien for another year, threw in his lot with the southern workers when they moved to Tennessee, stayed by the Madison School through its first year's experience, and was one of the first men to launch out into the starting of the hill school work. As much as money is needed in this southern work, men are needed more, and the fishing process, as it is often called, is considered successful not when it brings a few dollars into the work, but when one succeeds in landing men of mind and consecration.

California friends have not been the only ones to-help in this southern work, but they have certainly been generous. Another California brother s first donation was $100. Later he gave $500, with a promise of a thousand more. Several years after that, he showed his real zeal and earnestness for the southern work by sending one daughter to the school. Following that, he sent two more children. He visited the place himself, and on leaving promised the money to put up a sanitary cow barn with room for twenty-five cows.

(The school's capacity for students is about sixty. Two more cottages planned west of Gotzian Hall; two isolation cottages for contagious diseases; laboratory, office room. Sometimes crowded; two families have been in one room, five members of a family in another, five girls living in Phelps, four girls living in one room in another cottage.)

Donations of work have been received at various times. In 1905, Brethren Nelson, Jensen, Gotfredson, and Whittet, rendered valuable help in the buildings. The spirit of giving was sweetly manifested not long ago when one of the young women, whose home is across the continent, wrote her father that if he were willing she would give up her trip home for a vacation and donate the price of the trip to the fund being raised for a small laboratory for the science classes. This is by no means all. In every direction that one looks about the school, he sees evidences of friendly interest and concern. Are not people interested in the South? Many are, and have thrown out a line which is drawing them toward the South, and in time they themselves will be actively engaged in the great southern cause.

Students themselves sometimes make donations. One day Prof. Brailiar visited the school at Hillcrest and told the story of the starting of a small mission school for colored children by two of the students at Hillcrest. A man and his wife had left the Hillcrest School, had gone into Mississippi, and were struggling hard to pay for a small piece of land. The story appealed to the students, and opportunity was given them to show what they would like to do. In a very few minutes the price of a cow was

83

pledged. These pledges could not be paid at once; in fact, some of the students themselves had to write to their friends and solicit the money they had pledged. But the experience of either giving the money or raising it was good for them.

Later, when practically the same body of students heard the story of a colored girl who did not have money enough to travel to the Hillcrest School, but who gave promise of being a profitable student, they raised in about fifteen minutes the necessary money for transportation.

Two years ago the old farm bell, which had rung us to our meals and into bed and out of bed night and morning, fell and was broken. The bell was on the place when we purchased it, and it now became necessary to have a new one. The students themselves took up the matter, raised the money, purchased the bell, and erected an iron tower on which to hang it. This was one of the first memorials erected by students themselves.

In the spring of 1912, when the new dining hall was ready to be occupied, the question of furnishings arose. The chairs used in the dining rooms in Old Plantation were low, willow-bottomed chairs, purchased in the early days of the institution. The matter of new chairs for the new dining room was discussed by the student body, and it was voted in Union Meeting to raise the money for six dozen chairs at $2 apiece. Pledges were taken, some offering to raise the money for one chair, others for as high as six chairs.

This made it necessary for the students to write to their friends, for very few of them thought they could afford the price of a chair themselves. It gave them an opportunity to describe the work as they might not otherwise have described it. They told what was being done in the school, how furnishings have been secured in the past, and asked the help of their friends. The effort on the part of our students to raise money develops in them intellectual strength, conversion to a principle, and teaches them how to direct the attention of others to a field that needs help. There is no other single way better fitted for educating Seventh-day Adventists at a distance, than by telling them the story of the South and asking financial aid. The interest has not been confined entirely to our own people. This is illustrated by the donation of $50 worth of tools to the blacksmith shop by the firm of Montgomery Ward & Co. of Chicago, and the same amount by Sears, Roebuck, & Co.

The gift of giving has been tested in families in the development of some of the auxiliary schools. The land in one mountain school was purchased for a young man and his wife by his father. The mother of another young man disposed of her property in a northern city, and put all she could command into the development of the highland school work. Two lady canvassers, well-known in the denomination, Sisters Lackey and McDonald-Waters, have been largely responsible financially for another highland school in its infant days.

The biggest donations, however, or the ones that seem to count as the largest according to the Scripture standard, are the ones made by those men and women who, heeding God's call to the needy South, give themselves and their all, be that little or much. There are numerous lights burning in the South lit by just such sacrifices, and those are the lights that never grow dim.

Top: Carrie and Bessie DeGraw as students at Battle Creek, 1891–1892.
Bottom: Bessie DeGraw at Madison College, c. 1920.

CHAPTER 22

THE SANITARIUM AND SCHOOL

Very clear instruction has been given concerning the cooperation that should exist between a sanitarium and a school. The two institutions should be associated for the benefit of both. After speaking of the harmony that should exist between the work of the sanitarium and the school, the Spirit of Prophecy says,

> The benefits of hearty cooperation extend beyond physicians and teachers, students and sanitarium helpers. When a sanitarium is built near a school, those in charge of the educational institution have a grand opportunity of setting a right example before those who all through life have been easygoing idlers, and who have come to the sanitarium for treatment. The patients will see the contrast between the idle, self-indulgent life that they have lived, and the life of self-denial and service lived by Christ's followers. They will learn that the object of medical missionary work is to restore, to correct wrongs, to show human beings how to avoid the self-indulgence that brings disease and death.

> The words and actions of the workers in the sanitarium and in the school should plainly reveal that life is an intensely solemn thing, in view of the account which all must render to God.

Since the opening of the Rural Sanitarium, the results of this cooperation have been plainly seen. The patients at the sanitarium are often very impressed with the character of the workers. More than once they have been known to say that they have never met a class of young people having a more definite purpose in life. This one thing appears strongly to those who come in search of health.

The sanitarium patients are much interested in the development of the school. They become acquainted with the system of self-government, the industrial work, and other features of the school. Frequently they attend the Union Meetings. They can he found wandering over the farm where the young men are at work, they visit the garden from which the sanitarium table is supplied with vegetables, and the dairy, with whose products they have already become acquainted at the sanitarium. Their attention is called to the fact that the buildings are the work of the carpentry class, and this in itself appeals strongly to men and women who are interested in practical education. Each day at the sanitarium, worship is held in the chapel. From time to time, lectures are delivered on health topics, and the minds of the patients are directed to the importance of diet reform, correct habits of living and thinking, the value of the simple life, the reasons for establishing a sanitarium in the country, etc. The home life of many of these patients has been changed as the result of their stay at the sanitarium. They become acquainted with the unique ideas of the Seventh-day Adventists through conversation with nurses and physicians, by attending Sabbath services with the school family, and through religious meetings which are held in the sanitarium itself. Each Sabbath evening when the weather is favorable, the vesper service for the entire school family is held on the sanitarium lawn. For some time, it has been the custom of physicians, nurses, and workers to hold a daily prayer service for the patients and the work in general.

Thinking men and women are among the patients; businessmen spend their vacations here; writers of note have been patients. And as these people come in contact with the busy life of the institution, they are often deeply impressed, and express themselves as intensely interested in the principles which are being worked out in the institution. A very hearty spirit of cooperation has also been shown by physicians of Nashville, a number of leading physicians and surgeons sending patients to the institution. At various times, surgical work has been done here by Nashville physicians, and this, added to the influence gained as a result of taking medical work in Vanderbilt University by Prof. Sutherland and Prof. Magan, has made it possible for these principles to become more widely known than under any other conditions.

At one time, it was thought the Rural Sanitarium was located at too great a distance from the city to work with any advantage in the city, but since the building of the new road on the school farm and the improvement of the county road, Nashville can easily be reached within twenty minutes by automobile, and it is not an unusual thing for the sanitarium to be visited by from six to a dozen automobile parties in a day.

The Madison Sanitarium is a very small institution, but its very simplicity is in its favor. Each patient is dealt with individually. He comes daily in contact with physicians and helpers in a way that the patients in a larger sanitarium cannot. The institution maintains the closest cooperation between school and sanitarium workers. In the case of the Madison School and the Rural Sanitarium, we have not two institutions. The sanitarium is simply a department of the school. The members of the school faculty are physicians, matrons, and helpers in the sanitarium. The nurses trained to carry the work at the sanitarium receive their training under these same physicians and other instructors in the school. They work a part of their time in the sanitarium and a part in other parts of the school. There is absolutely no division between the sanitarium workers and the rest of the student body.

From a missionary viewpoint, we feel that there is an advantage in having those who need help to seek it by coming to us, rather than to depend upon having the workers seek out those who need the help. Those who have been physically benefited usually have hearts that are responsive to the truth. The Savior's life illustrates this method of missionary work. One well-known lady who had been a patient here came to the institution against the wishes of her friends, because they feared she would be indoctrinated. When she returned to her home, she was asked how much she was preached to, and her answer was, "They do not need to preach; they live their religion."

Nurses who have received their training at the Madison Sanitarium are in constant demand for private work in the city, and are frequently called by city physicians, when they can he spared from the home institution. They have been the bedside attendants in some of the best-known families in the city. It is through the influence of the sanitarium that the way is gradually opening for a more extended work in the city itself.

Top: Sanitarium patients and nurses on the porch of the Sanitarium.
Bottom: E. A. Sutherland (center of middle row) with students.

CHAPTER 23

THE FARM

The location of the farm has been mentioned in the story of finding the place. Writing to Elder Daniells on June 13, 1904, when Sister White and her party were taking their river trip up the Cumberland, she said, "We wish to visit a farm at Madison. . . It is said that this farm contains nearly 100 acres of quality agricultural land suitable for grain and fruit, and about 200 acres of pasture land." Later she said, "We went once more to see the farm, after its purchase had been completed, and were very much pleased with it."

Nearly five years later, in April 1909, in addressing the student body, Sister White said, "When I first visited Madison about five years ago and looked over this school property, I told those who were with me that in appearance it was similar to one of the places that had been presented before me in vision during the night season: a place where our people would have opportunity of presenting the light of truth to those who had never heard the last gospel message." And, after telling of the work that should be done on this farm, she said, "This beautiful farm at Madison is a means of support."

The Madison farm at first appeared to those who purchased it as a rocky, uncomfortable piece of property. Compared with farms in the Mississippi Valley and corn land in Iowa and Illinois, it seemed to present a decidedly hard proposition to self-supporting workers. On the other hand, the Spirit of Prophecy speaks of it as a beautiful farm. It is well-wooded, the timber being principally oak, maple, locust, walnut, hackberry, red cedar, and elm. It lies on the banks of the Cumberland River. The river touches what is known as 200 acres on the south side, then makes a long bend known as Neely's Bend, a distance of twelve miles to the point where it touches the farm again on the opposite side.

The amount of pastureland makes it advisable to raise cattle, and for the maintenance of the dairy, the principal crops have been feed crops, such as corn, sorghum cane, cowpeas, clover, etc. Ten acres of upland lying east of Old Plantation House is the garden, where vegetables of all kinds are raised, supplying the needs of the school family and the sanitarium family. The oversupply is at times sold in Nashville, but no effort is made to raise vegetables for the market. Beans, sweet corn, tomatoes, beets, and okra are canned for winter use. The garden was largely developed by Sister Margaret Lanker, who came to the school in 1906 from College View, Nebraska. Her energy was devoted to the development of that phase of the school work, and she will always be remembered as one of those self-sacrificing workers who had a part in the pioneer movement.

About fifty acres of the rough land has been fenced for sheep and goats. Goats prove advantageous to the place in clearing up the underbrush, and the school has experimented with them for the sake of encouraging students who purchase property in highland districts where much of the land needs to be cleared.

The attention of the workers has always been drawn to the experience at Avondale, Australia, and the farm at Madison is similar to the Avondale school farm. To many it seemed unpromising, but the Lord saw in it things that men did not see.

> There is a work to be done for young men and women that is not yet accomplished. There are much larger numbers of young people who need to have the advantages of our training schools. They need the manual training course that will teach them how to lead an active, energetic life. All kinds of labor must be connected with our schools. Under wise, judicious, God-fearing directors, the students are to be taught. Every branch of the work is to be conducted in the most thorough and systematic ways that long experience and wisdom can enable us to plan and execute. Let the teachers wake up to the importance of this subject, and teach agriculture and other industries that it is essential for the students to understand. Look in every department of labor to reach the very best results.

> Let the science of the Word of God be brought into the work, that the students may understand correct principles, and may reach the highest

possible standard. Exert your God-given abilities, and bring all your energies into the development of the Lord's farm. Study and labor, that the best results and the greatest returns may come from the seed-sowing, that there may be an abundant supply of food, both temporal and spiritual, for the increased number of students that shall be gathered in to be trained as Christian workers.

The farm has been considered the Lord's farm. We are told that it should continually teach parables, that it is to become a great object lesson, not only to the students themselves, but to the community. It is to be made a park. An attempt has been made to follow this instruction. The very first work of the institution was to study the farm and farm conditions carefully, and to begin a course of action which would make the farm the basis for support in the school.

It is the custom in this community for Negro laborers to do the greater part of the work on the soil. On the Madison School farm, practically all the work has been done by students and teachers working together. When the farm was first purchased, Prof. Sutherland and Prof. Magan took their turns as farm manager. Later, Bro. Chas. Kendall acted as farm manager for two years; and when Bro. Kendall felt the time had come for him to establish a school of his own (which he did in Arkansas), Bro. W. F. Rocke became the farm manager.

The farm and the farm work constitute one of the three main activities of the institution. The other two are the normal training department and the sanitarium. When purchased, the farm was in a decidedly rundown condition. It had been owned by men who had regularly followed a one-crop plan of cultivation. Large yields of wheat had been taken from certain fields until the fertility of the land was exhausted, and in places was badly washed out. Year by year this worn land has been brought to a higher state of fertility by being allowed to rest by the raising of nitrogen-producing crops and by a thorough system of cultivation, etc. Particular attention has been given to the study of agriculture, not only by the teachers, but by a large number of the students.

Very valuable assistance has been given by Prof. K. A. Morgan, State Director of Farmers' Institutes and by other instructors in the Agricultural

College of the University at Knoxville. Regular studies have been conducted, using the farmer's bulletins issued by the United States Department of Agriculture, as well as by the literature of the State Department.

For some time, the State Department has desired to conduct an experiment station on the school farm, but no active steps were taken in that direction until the summer of 1912, when arrangements were made to carry on experimental work on three acres of land selected by the state's representative; one-half to be cultivated and fertilized according to the state's direction, and one-half to demonstrate the value of green manuring.

There was practically no fruit on this place when it was purchased, and some felt that fruit could not be raised in this section, owing to the adverse experience of many who had made the attempt. However, early in the experience of the school, 500 trees were set out on a piece of rolling land on the west side of the farm. A small vineyard was started at the same time. Later, another orchard was planted northeast of the campus. In the orchard are to be found apples, peaches, plums, prunes, pears, cherries. An experiment is being made with the raising of pecans. The Miller Nursery, of Milton, Ore., donated sweet cherries.

An orchard in Tennessee has many enemies to contend with. The state is neither a northern nor a southern state so far as climate is concerned, and the late spring frosts make some fruit crops uncertain. Insect pests are numerous, and the most careful attention must be given to the culture of trees. The Experiment Station at Nashville has cooperated with the school in the care of the orchard, and Prof. Keiffer has made several visits to the school in the interest of that work.

CHAPTER 24

LIVESTOCK

When the farm was purchased, there came with it about seventy head of cattle and sixty hogs. Early in October 1904, the hogs were sold. Mrs. Druillard herself delivered them to the stockyards in Nashville. This occasioned a good deal of merriment, because it was a most unusual thing for a woman to do such business in the South, and the stockman made the remark that he would predict success for the institution which had such a woman as its business manager.

Many of the cattle were suitable only for beef, and arrangements were made to sell them. The agreement was that the school should deliver the part of the herd that had to be sold, at the corner where Neely's Bend Road joins Gallatin Pike, two miles from the school. Many of the cattle were so wild that when the attempt was made to drive them, it was almost impossible to get them to the pike. One animal had to be shot, another fell and broke her leg, and before the herd finally reached Nashville, another cow had lost her life at a railway crossing.

It was then decided to build up the herd gradually. The men on the farm, accustomed to a large breed of cattle, decided that the wisest course would be to purchase a general-purpose breed. Prof. Magan and Bro. Brink made a memorable trip into the country sixty miles north of Nashville, in search of cows, and the first addition to the Madison school dairy consisted of a separator was purchased in the early history of the dairy, and a little later a Babcock tester. Active experiments were conducted in order to determine whether the cows were profitable.

It was soon found that many of the cows were eating their heads off. Gradually the older herd was disposed of and a beginning was made in building up a Jersey herd. The first purchase was of five animals from the well-known Gardner herd in Nashville, descendants of Jersey cattle imported by Mr. Hood of the Hood's Sarsaparilla Co. in Massachusetts. Careful and continuous study of the dairy business was made by the school. The proper feed for the cows, balanced ration, and proper care and grooming of the milk cows were all subjects for study and discussion. Milk records were procured and frequent tests made of the percentage of butterfat in each cow's milk. In this way, a definite record was kept of the cost of each animal and the income from the sale of her butter.

The Jersey cattle were paid for with the butter they produced. For the first year or more, the butter of the N.A.N.I. was delivered in pound rolls, in paper bearing the school label, at one of the leading hotels of the city. Later, the entire school supply was taken by one of the grocery men, who had his regular patrons for the butter from the school dairy. Miss DeGraw was the deliveryman in those days. She drove to town, always with a little tan mule who had his idiosyncrasies. Stiff-bitted, he obeyed nothing but his own will, and took his own sweet way at his own chosen pace, o'er hill and dale, and through city streets. Going downhill, the cart would push him, and he would break into a trot, faster and faster, till the ascent of the next hill stopped him, and up that he would slowly poke. No pulling would stop him, and no pounding drive him. Doubtless he was a philosopher, for he knew the tender inexperience of his driver; so, unheeding but sagacious, he threaded his safe way around the carts of the marketplace and always deposited his treasures safely at the backdoor of the hotel. Here Miss DeGraw delivered her butter, eggs, and chickens; then, driving around to the front door and shedding her coat, would walk in the main entrance to get her money and be invited by the proprietor to take dinner.

At present the herd consists of a large number of registered cows and grade cows. In later years, with a large sanitarium family and a growing school family, a large part of the butter and cream has been used to supply home needs. The school has been able to assist quite a few other schools in introducing a strain of thoroughbred Jerseys into their communities.

Brother Brink was the first member of the school family to live on the place. He came in June 1904, to take charge of the stock. He has held that position faithfully for eight years. It is almost impossible to induce him to leave the farm for a week at a time. When he goes away, it is to visit some other dairy or to spend a little time at the agricultural college, better to fit himself for his work. No more devoted laborer can be found in the company.

The barns used by the school up to the present time were on the place when it was purchased. These have been repaired, it is true, but the young men who have worked in the school dairy have been obliged to operate under practically the same conditions here that they are called upon to deal with when they go out into their own little schools, and have to make use of the things they find with but a limited amount of money for improvements.

The dairy was not only the principal means of support for the school during the first years of its existence, and before the sanitarium was established, but it was also a valuable advertisement for the school, which offered students an opportunity to make their way by working and helped in training teachers to establish rural industrial schools in places which the South itself greatly recognizes as much in need of this form of educational work.

Nellie Druillard with three women in an automobile at Madison College. Photo taken in 1915.

CHAPTER 25

POULTRY AND BEES

It was felt by those who were first on the farm in the year 1904, that poultry raising could be made a success. The enterprise began by the purchase of half a dozen hens from a neighbor in the Bend. The company of workers was small in those days, and every man and every woman on the place took his or her part in the actual work of the institution.

The minutes show that Bro. Orin Wolcott was the first gardener and Bro. Calvin Kinsman did the mechanical work about the place; then, when poultry-raising was decided upon, Miss DeGraw was made head of the department. A 250-egg incubator was purchased; and since there was no suitable place for it, one corner of the south porch was boarded in for a broad house, and the first hatch of chickens was watched, just outside the chapel window, with the greatest delight by every member of the family. The department has been maintained, the policy being to raise about three or four hundred chickens each year.

A few colonies of bees have been maintained on the school farm, producing honey for home consumption, but no special effort has been made in this direction. The success of the bees depends largely upon the season, which regulates the number and variety of honey-producing flowers.

Three men posing on the porch of an early campus building.

CHAPTER 26

CARPENTRY

The students have been taught to raise their own crops, *to build their own houses*, and to care wisely for cattle and poultry
    — *words used by Sister White in describing the work of the Madison School*

The building work of the institution has been carried on gradually and done to benefit students who needed an education in carpentry. The institution has been favored with capable men as directors in this department, and a large number of students have received a practical training, which has been invaluable to them when they have gone into schools of their own. Bro. Calvin Kinsman, one of the first to associate with the school at Madison, did a large part of the work on one or two of the first cottages, and as a result of the experience he gained, he largely made his way on the island of Cuba while he was learning the language.

The instruction in carpentry is given in the form of classwork, and the practical experience and demonstration on the building itself. Among the students who have worked in this department and have carried responsibility in this work are Bro. Arthur Hall, John Samson, Rolla Snyder, and Wellesley Magan, who came to the school as a boy of twelve and worked on a large number of buildings, developing skill in carpentry, painting, and general woodwork.

Two unknown men in front of the college carpentry shop.

CHAPTER 27

BLACKSMITHING AND REPAIR WORK

T he first horseshoeing and repair work of the institution was done in one room of Probation Hall by Bro. Calvin Kinsman. The grindstone stood outside the door, and the tools were sharpened there. After Bro. Kinsman went to Cuba, this kind of work was carried on by Bro. Sweeten.

In 1909, Bro. Claud Rouse became the blacksmith for the institution. A small shop was built on the barn lot and furnished with a forge and a few simple tools. Bro. Rouse is a genius when it comes to repair work, and he came and went at the beck and call of everybody on the place, doing, it would seem, anything that needed to be done, from sharpening scissors to putting tires on a wagon or guttering on a house. Bro. Rouse left in 1911, and the blacksmith work passed into the hands of a Bro. Black.

In council with members of the faculty, Bro. Black decided to make a tour in the interests of the work, soliciting means for the building of more commodious quarters. Bro. Black had been a student in the school for one year. He was deeply interested in the development of the mechanical work, and while this was the first time a student teacher had ever attempted to raise money for the school, he was willing to undertake the job. He spent several weeks in the winter of 1911-12 in the North, visiting relatives, and old schoolmates. He was blessed to a wonderful degree in this undertaking, and succeeded in raising, in money and pledges, a sufficient amount to build a shop 24 x 48.

He himself put in a strong foundation, and with the help of some of these young men of the carpentry class, put up the building, a story and a half, with gambrel roof, the upper part to be used for storage, the lower part to be divided into blacksmith shop and carpenter shop.

Bro. Black found many people interested in the work. Soliciting donations gave him an experience he could not have gained in any other way. He was helped by our own people, and while in Chicago felt that he should present the work to some of the firms that handled such tools as would be needed in the shop. He was given an opportunity to talk with the managers of both Montgomery Ward and Sears Roebuck, & Co, and both firms responded with a donation of $50 worth of tools.

It is the purpose, when the shop is finished and equipped, to give students an opportunity to make furniture for school purposes, as well as give an opportunity for other lines of work which could not be carried on without a shop. It is decided to make tables for the dining room. The boys' rooms have always had little furniture; they have been promised that just as soon as the shop is ready, they shall have opportunity to make their own.

CHAPTER 28

BOARDING

When the family was first organized, in October 1904, meals were served on the American plan, in the southeast room of the Old Plantation House. Later that room was made the school's sitting room, and a larger room, the north room on the front of the building, became the dining room. Still later both these rooms were utilized, up to the time of the completion of the new dining room in the summer of 1912.

The school was only a few months old when it was voted in Union Meeting to change from the American to the European plan of service. The kitchen was small, there was no serving room, and the form of service at the table was accommodated to these conditions. Instead, therefore, of serving each person in small dishes, as is usually done where the European plan is followed, eight people sat at each table, one gentleman serving as host, one lady as hostess.

Meals were ordered one day, to be served the next. Instead of being put in individual dishes, vegetables were served in large dishes, and all orders of bread were served together. The hostess read the menu, and the host served each person according to her directions. This was a combination of the European plan and the American plan which has proved decidedly satisfactory. There is a family spirit at the table, and there is opportunity to cultivate the power of service. Foods are served warmer and in better condition than on the purely European plan, and time is saved in the serving room. In this way, and also by each table's becoming responsible for the clearing of its own dishes, each host and hostess is held responsible for the comfort of those at his or her table.

In general, the food is served at the rate of two cents per order, the size of the order being determined by the market price. Four slices of bread always constitutes an order. A pound of butter is divided into 16 squares: an order therefore weighing an ounce. It has been the purpose of the department to make the prime just as low as possible, paying the actual cost of the food and the price of service. Students are paid for their work at the rate of ten cents per hour, and in return they are expected to pay for their meals, their room rent, their fuel and oil, and their laundry. The school issues a book of coupons in five-cent, two-cent, and one-cent pieces, and with this paper money all regular expenses about the institution are met. When meals are ordered, each individual calculates the expense of his order and pays for it with coupons. The menu blanks are gathered, the coupons counted, and a total of the orders from all tables is given to the kitchen. Based on this total, the cook gets her instruction for the meals for the next day. From it the gardener determines the kind and amount of vegetables to be delivered at the kitchen door and the bakers ascertain the amount of bread needed; that is delivered at the bread table. The woman in charge of the cream house furnishes the required amount of cream and butter.

The meals served are simple, consisting largely of the products of the garden in their season, the canned goods from the garden in wintertime, and such staple articles as beans, rice, corn in various forms, as well as various other preparations. An effort has always been made to keep on hand a supply of wholesome yeast bread. From the Dixie bakery, the school supplies itself with crackers and nut foods. The amount of fruit used is determined by the amount raised on the place, to which has been added from year to year the generous donations of friends in the West. There were times in the early history of the school when the variety of foods was decidedly limited. The farm was not raising fruit, there was very little cash income from students, and the school was dependent almost entirely for fruit upon donations. Prunes may be considered a boarding-house dish, but there have been times when prunes were welcomed as one of the most delicious articles of food that could be asked for. The school has usually been fortunate enough to raise a good many tomatoes, which are canned. In good years the strawberry crop has yielded fruit for the winter. The country produces excellent wild strawberries, and it is an unusual year when these have not been canned in quantities.

A strict department account is kept by the institution's bookkeeper, so that it is definitely known whether or not there is a deficit in the department. The dairy products have always served as a very substantial basis for supplying the tables, even though other foods were limited. As the orchard begins to bear and it is possible to raise a larger variety of food on the farm and in the garden and to can a larger amount of foods, we want to reduce the amount of dairy products used.

The story of some of the reforms that have been advocated from time to time, and some of the studies that have been given along diet reform during the history of the institution, constitute an interesting chapter, if the details could be given. There have been times when it was thought the food was lacking in protein; this would lead to a study of foods and food combinations. The use of unleavened bread was advocated strongly by Sister Gotzian during her life in the institution, and members of the family still recall the rolls she taught students to make. Occasionally someone advocated very strongly that all milk products should be discarded.

That person, of course, is allowed to follow his own inclination in this matter. At various times in the history of the institution, certain boarders have substituted olive oil or some other fat for butter and possibly for cream. The general policy of the school has been to furnish staple articles in orders just as large as the market price would permit, to discourage the use of desserts and foods that require soda or baking powder, rich pastry, and a large amount of milk, sugar, and eggs in combination, and to utilize as far as possible the foods raised on the place, and so to prepare in an appetizing form the food that will appear on the tables, and to limit the variety at each meal but to vary the articles served from meal to meal.

The cooking for the school family has been done throughout the history of the school by students, usually by young women. It is the plan to hold one young woman responsible for the breakfast and another for the dinner, giving her such additional help as she needs. The serving of the meals, the care of the dining room, the washing of dishes, the baking of bread, the canning of the fruit: these lines of work have in general been carried by the young women under the direction of the teachers. From time to time regular classes have been conducted in hygienic cooking. This is made part of the instruction offered in the nurses' class. It is one of the regular lines of work given in the short course, and aside from that the matron is expected to function as teacher along these and other lines of domestic science as the young women come into that department. The work of this department, as well as all other departments in which the young women work, is brought week by week to the attention of the entire women's department at its department meetings, and a general report from the department is given each week at the Union Meeting. In this way, the workings of the department come before the student body. It is the privilege of any student to question the service, or to make suggestions that will improve the workings of the domestic science department. The aim is to make the work educational, while at the same time affording young lady students an opportunity to meet school expenses by work. In this department, as in all others, the general outline of the work is put into the form of department rules, and each young woman, as she enters the department, is expected to familiarize herself with those rules. Failure to carry out the rules of the department subject one to correction, reprimand, or possibly a fine in the department meetings.

CHAPTER 29

SCHOOL POLICIES

In speaking of the Madison School, the Spirit of Prophecy calls it a training school for home and foreign missionary teachers. The main object in the minds of the founders of the institution was to establish a school which would enable people in the North would[sic] become acquainted with the great southern field, and in which those who have become interested in this field might be prepared for active, practical missionary work. It has been made plain to Seventh-day Adventists that every school should be located on a farm, and those students should have an opportunity to receive a practical agricultural training.

> They need the manual training course that will teach them how to lead an active, energetic life. All kinds of labor must be connected with our schools. Let the teachers wake up to the importance of this subject, and teach agriculture and other industries that it is essential for students to understand. [Testimonies]Vol. VI, page 191.

This is sufficient reason for the establishment of a school to include the agricultural features of the work which are suggested by its name. The school was set by the Spirit of Prophecy to train missionary teachers; therefore, the normal phase of school work ought to be developed. "It is essential that there shall be a sanitarium connected with the Madison School. The educational work at the school and the sanitarium can go forward hand in hand." It therefore became necessary to develop the medical missionary phase of the work. From the foregoing quotations one can determine the three leading features of the Madison School. It is an agricultural school, a normal school, and a school emphasizing medical missionary work. These indicate the course of instruction offered. The plan of work to be followed was not entirely new to the company of teachers when they began the work at Madison. Much thought had been given to these three distinct phases of education even before the moving of Battle Creek College. In Berrien Springs, still further attention had been given to these same educational ideas, and when the school opened at Madison, the policy itself was fairly well-defined.

> I have been shown that in our educational work, we are not to follow the methods that have been adopted in our older established schools. There is among us too much clinging to old customs, and because of this we are far behind where we should be in the development of the Third Angel's Message. Because men could not comprehend the purpose of God in the plans laid before us for the education of the workers, methods have been followed in some of our schools which have retarded rather than advanced the work of God. Years have passed into eternity with small results that might have shown the accomplishment of a great work.

Such instruction has made it seem necessary to study very carefully the methods of instruction to be pursued, and the general plan for developing the work at Madison.

The work at Madison.

Three things had to be kept in mind: the manual work of the institution was to be done by students. For this they must have time. The intellectual work must be of such a character that students will not be held in school year after year, but must be prepared in a short time to do an effective work. And while those two ideas were carried out, the standard of the work must be elevated rather than lowered.

The school has been small, dealing with from 20 students the first year to 70 during the last year, so that it has been possible to deal with individual needs of its students in a way that could not be done in a large school. In order to carry on the manual work, making it profitable to both the student and the institution, classwork has been arranged so that a student can devote one-half day to manual work and one half a day to intellectual work.

The day's program runs about as follows:

> Milking bell, 5 a.m.
> Breakfast, 6 a.m.
> Worship, 6:45 a.m.

Manual work, 7:15 a.m. to 12:45 p.m. for a part of the students, and at 10:00 am, class period for another division.

Dinner, 1 p.m.

Manual work and class, 2 p.m. and 3 p.m. to 6 p.m.

Chores, 6 to 7 p.m.

Chapel period, 7:15 to 8 p.m.

Evening study, 8 to 9:30 p.m.

Retiring, 9:30 p.m.

A student enters the school desiring to make his school expenses by work. He is assigned work in one of the industrial departments. His work is outlined for him; he familiarizes himself with the rules of the department, and carries on his work in counsel with the instructor or a student who has the oversight of the work in that department. The character of his work is noted; punctuality is expected, a teachable spirit makes advancement possible, and at the end of each quarter he is given a grade, showing the character of the work he has done. Each day he reports the amount of time spent in manual labor, giving himself credit at the rate of ten cents per hour. At the end of each month he makes out a time slip showing the work done. This is supposed to agree with his daily time slips, which are on file in the business office. From the total amount of work done be subtracts what is known as his two-hour time, which is equivalent to twenty cents a day for six days in the week, and for the remainder he receives credit on school expenses.

The class work of this same student is arranged according to his individual needs. A person who intends to become a nurse and needs preparatory work is advised to enter one of the preparatory classes. One who has made up his mind to become a teacher is directed into the classes which will qualify him for that kind of work.

The classwork in this institution is carried on in a somewhat different way from that in many other institutions, although the Madison School is not alone in what is known as the one-study plan. Each student carries one main intellectual subject. This plan calls for a three-hour recitation period, during which time the class recites in one subject under one teacher. By this plan, the student covers in one term a single subject, which under the ordinary plan he would take a year to cover; and thus in one year he takes on the whole as many studies as by the usual plan. The one-study plan has been severely tested, and its value proved by many years' experience. Students well-qualified to do the work in a training school find it to their advantage to concentrate their energies upon one line of work until they have completed it. Many of the students entering the school desire to do intensive work in certain lines, completing in as short a time as possible a definite amount of work. The one-study plan makes that possible. To get the best results from class work, the method known as "correlation" has been advocated for many years by the best educators. The one-study plan makes it possible for the teacher to correlate as no other plan can. A class in English grammar, for instance, is given an opportunity not only in the technical study, but in such work as he may need in reading, writing, spelling, composition, observational studies, nature studies, etc. Science classes conducted on the one-study plan combine technical work with laboratory work. Nurses' classes combine bookwork and practical demonstration of the subject in the sanitarium bathrooms.

The day's work is practically closed with the evening chapel. This part of the day's work is placed in the evening, in order that every student may attend. Prompt and regular attendance is required of both teachers and students. During this chapel period, various educational matters are handled. A Bible study or a study of educational principles is conducted. This is followed by a Union Meeting, by a social and prayer meeting, by a study of current events, or by some other exercise which calls into play the intellect of the student and offers him an opportunity to acquaint himself with the principles upon which the school is conducted.

There is no one place where students do their studying. There is one hour when all the student body study their lessons. It is impossible to arrange for these with work carried on as it is in the institution. Each student is expected to make a program for himself and to follow that program. He is here, not as a child that needs to be guided in every particular, but as a man or woman capable of taking the initiative, of bearing responsibility, and of being self-governing.

CHAPTER 30

FREE TUITION

No tuition charge is made to students of the N.A.N.I. The question of free tuition in our schools was first considered in a council meeting in Berrien Springs, in the year 1902, when a number of General Conference and Lake Union Conference officers met with the faculty of Emmanuel Missionary College, and plans were laid for conducting a ministerial institute. At that time it was arranged that men should be brought in from the field for a short course at the college. They were to be given free tuition, because they were active laborers, and it was felt that if the state can educate its children free of charge, the church or the conference ought to be willing to do as much for its laborers. This was the beginning of the free tuition plan.

When the work was started at Madison, it was for students, every one of whom was supposed to be a candidate for active work in the southern field. The institution does not bid for any other class of students, and with this idea in mind, it has always offered free tuition. In fact, the expenses of the student are put at the very lowest figures possible, and an opportunity is given a large number each year to make up those expenses by labor, so that nothing need stand in the way of a consecrated young man or woman who desires an education in order to fit himself to become a laborer in the southern field.

Free tuition puts the student in a place where he feels under obligation to the institution. The institution gives its life for the building up of the work. In return it asks that that each student shall live out the principles according to which he has been educated and shall carry out to the best of his ability those same principles in his future work, either as a medical missionary, an industrial school teacher, a canvasser, a minister, or whatever else his line of work may be.

Free tuition has been made possible in the Madison School from the fact that the school is located on a farm, where much of the expense other schools bear is avoided by its raising its own produce. The number of workers has always been small in proportion to the amount of work done, not because the institution has not needed more teachers, but because it has not been in a position to offer wages to teachers; this is the exception rather than the rule, when men and women are willing to take up this kind of work on the basis on which the teachers of the Madison School have labored. Teachers working for their board and room, as they have done in Madison, have a right to expect a great deal from their students; the only reward for the efforts these teachers put forth, is in seeing students leave the institution inspired with the needs of the southern cause, and filled with a desire to devote their lives to this cause.

The Spirit of Prophecy has said more than once that the education given at Madison fits students "to go forth as self-supporting missionaries." The teachers have reasoned that if students are to become self-supporting workers when they leave the Madison School, they must be given an opportunity to be self-supporting in the school. If they are to be self-supporting in the school, they must have before them the example of teachers who are willing to sacrifice, to restrict their wants, and to work not for a wage, but for the good of the cause. They have therefore been content with that original $13 a month, awaiting the time when the school, through the farm or the sanitarium, may be able to give them a little higher wage.

Various institutions have found that where the industries are given due prominence and where students are encouraged to become self-supporting, self-government naturally develops. There is something about this form of education which makes it possible to organize the students and the teachers into a cooperative body. The Madison School has as its object the training of workers. A worker who goes out tomorrow to control others must be able today to look after himself. If he expects to be able to take the initiative in a work of his own, he must be able to take the initiative in the parent institution. If he is to be a burden-bearer anywhere in the world, he needs to be a burden-bearer in the institution that is giving him every opportunity to fit himself for his lifework. There are various companies and organizations in the world which teach students to be self-governing in a civil sense. Schools have been organized on the plan of city government; but this Madison School is considered a religious organization, and the basic principle for discipline is outlined in Matthew 18:15-17. The idea is to throw upon the student the responsibility of making the laws, and then to throw the responsibility of seeing that the rules are properly obeyed also upon him. Each man, in a sense, becomes his brother's keeper. In matters of discipline it works this way: cases which in other circumstances are handled by the faculty, are in the Madison School handled either by the students themselves, where they are settled in a quiet way, or else, if the case becomes aggravated, it is brought before the Union Body. There is no such thing as the faculty standing on one side of a subject and the student body on the opposite side, for the two bodies are working together. Members of the faculty are subject to the rules of the institution, and are a part of the Union Body in the same way that each student is.

Home of Edward and Sallie Sutherland.
Photo c. 1915

CHAPTER 31

THE CLASS OF STUDENTS

The large majority of the students who have attended the N.A.N.I. have come from the East, the West, and the North. When the school was first established, there was a little feeling that it might draw students who should attend the Graysville School, and so no special effort has ever been made to draw students from the southern states. In fact, the object of the school is to interest people at a distance in the southern field, and bring into this field those whom the Spirit of the Lord indicates when it says that hundreds of Seventh-day Adventist families should locate in the South.

Some of the students have been brought into the school as a result of the personal work of some of the teachers at camp meetings and elsewhere. Others have been interested through literature that has been sent to them from the school. A good deal of work has been done along this line by correspondence, and during the past two years the students of the school have carried on an active campaign to interest their friends in the South. Through this means, people in a great many places have been led to read of the Madison School and of the situation in the South, and as their attention is directed to this field, the Spirit of the Lord brings conviction, and from time to time these individuals apply to enter the school. It is in these ways that the student body is recruited. It is not unusual for a man and his wife, and sometimes several children, to come into the school as students. At one time, a minister from California and his wife who had been a teacher In former years came to Madison with three children old enough to enter the school. It is by such families as this that several of the little hill schools have been started.

The building up of a faculty in such a school as the one at Madison is a different matter from the hiring of a faculty in an ordinary school. The first little company who were united in the enterprise divided the work among themselves. Each man taught or carried a full line of manual work, according to his ability or according to the demand made by students. With but a few students, and carrying out the one-study plan, the question of a teaching force is very much simplified. When the organization was perfected and a board of managers elected, it became the duty of the Board of Managers to legally provide the faculty. To select a faculty, however, in an institution where no inducement whatever in the form of wages is offered, is a delicate matter.

In various ways, the Spirit of the Lord has brought to the school men and women of ability. Some have come as students, and after spending a few months in the school, they have revealed teaching ability, together with a willingness to unite with the original teachers so far as finances are concerned. The management has never been in a position to make a general call for teachers. It has had to take them as they were presented. In the year 1910-11 the teaching force seemed decidedly weak, and a junior faculty was organized. This junior faculty was made up of some of the most capable students in the institution, each of whom was made responsible for some definite line of work in the institution. For instance, the man who had charge of the poultry was made a member of the junior faculty, likewise the man who had charge of the mechanical work. Years ago, the Spirit of Prophecy instructed our schools to educate students to do tutor work, and some of the classes in the school were carried by those who were otherwise students. And these student teachers were made members of the junior faculty. The junior faculty had the privilege of meeting with the senior members, studying the problems of the school with them; they had a voice in all the faculty meetings; they stood, as it were, between the student body and the faculty. It put them in a place where they had to take their stand definitely for the principles of the institution. They had to show that they were men and women capable of commanding the respect of their fellow-students. From this junior faculty, the Board of Managers was able to choose several teachers who later became members of the regular faculty.

It is difficult, in a place of this kind, to take a person who has been connected with an institution of a different type, and expect of him the same kind of work rendered by those who have been brought up in this institution. For that reason, it has been found advisable, insofar as possible, to educate our own workers here. As the young men and women who carry the burdens at the sanitarium are the product of the school, so our teaching force has been built up largely from those who have spent one or more years as students in the institution.

Each year four terms of work are offered by the school. Each year a strong line of Bible and Bible history is given. Each year a nurses' class is conducted, and it is from the nurses' class that the workers at the sanitarium are drawn. During the summer term, each year special attention is given to normal work and the preparation of teachers for highland schools. At intervals throughout the year, short courses are conducted in such subjects as agriculture, gardening, horseshoeing, blacksmithing, cooking, sewing, domestic science, etc.

THE RURAL SANITARIUM
Madison, Tennessee

Offers--

Airy, quiet rooms, each on the ground floor, spacious verandas for out-of-door living, physiologic-therapeutic treatment and hygienic dietary

At the following rates:-

Board and room, two meals per day, per week	- - - - -	$ 7.00
Board, room, and treatment (treatment daily except Sabbath), per week		15.00
Single meals,	- - - -	.35
Lodging, per night,	- - - -	.50
Day nurse (10 hours) per week,	-	15.00
Night nurse (10 hours) per week,	-	15.00
Bath-room treatments,	- -	1.00-2.00
General examination	- - -	5.00
Laboratory examination	- -	Extra
Hack to or from Madison Station,	-	.50
Baggage to or from Madison Station,		.25

You are cordially invited to visit the Rural Sanitarium and see for yourself what the institution offers, or for information, call N. H. Druillard, telephone Walnut 1312 L.

An undated advertising postcard for the Madison Sanitarium, c. 1920.

CHAPTER 32

CONVENTIONS

At the close of each summer school since the year 1908, there has been held a convention of self-supporting workers. This brings together representatives from the different schools, patrons of the Madison School and others who are interested in the study of the South and educational problems. These conventions differ from year to year, but the one held in August 1911, will serve to show the spirit of the work.

The convention opened Friday evening. The Sabbath was spent in appropriate services, social meetings, etc. On Sunday the work of the various small schools was discussed, the problems to be met in these schools were studied, and committees dealing with individual problems made their reports. Monday was Agricultural Day. A number of speakers were present, representing the state agricultural department and the agricultural college at Knoxville.

The superintendent of Davidson County gave the students an interesting address on industrial education. Miss Mary Hannah Johnson, of Knoxville, who has worked up a deep interest in libraries for rural districts, presented her favorite theme. It was a day full of interesting matter for those who are actively engaged in school work in highland districts.

Monday was devoted to medical missionary work and city mission work. The conference presidents of this union, Elder McVagh, president of the Southern Union Conference, the workers from the Nashville Sanitarium, and others who are connected with the work in Nashville and other portions of the South, were present. Dr. Paulson and Mrs. Clough of the Hinsdale Sanitarian were in attendance. Dr. Paulson gave some practical studies in city mission work, and there were a number of papers given on the general subject of city mission work and the relation of the country movement to the city mission.

At this time a committee was appointed, composed of members of the Southern Union Conference and representatives of the school, to study the needs of Nashville and to plan for cooperation in the city work. This committee considered the question from all sides; and since the last convention, in a very quiet way a number of young people from the Madison School have been canvassing and giving Bible readings in the city.

When the school was first established, on June 13, 1904, Sister White wrote Elder Daniells:

> We should enter at once upon the establishment in suitable places near Nashville of a school for white people and a school for colored people. The work in Nashville will gain influence from these working centers. The teachers in these schools can help the work in Nashville.

The sanitarium has been one avenue through which the school and its work have become known in the city of Nashville. It has been felt for a long time, however, that a mission should be started in the city, where students can spend a portion of their time and receive actual training in city mission work.

When the Madison School was opened, Elder Haskell and his wife had a Bible mission in the city. This, however, was closed while the school was still in its infancy, and Elder Haskell spent several years in California. It was hoped that Elder Haskell would return to Nashville to carry on city mission work, but, his desire to further the cause in the New England states has kept him out of the South. It was felt by the workers at Madison that the time had come to do something In the city. The question has been studied by the student body, and very earnest prayers have been offered for those who are working there in a quiet way, and that the Lord will open the way for someone to connect with this work who is able to conduct a mission. In the summer of 1912, while no mission has yet been opened, there are indications that the Lord has heard these prayers, and hearts have been turned to respond to the call for means to purchase the necessary property. It is hoped that the way will open for the development of this work in the near future.

CHAPTER 33

AUXILIARY SCHOOLS

It was at first the intention of the founders of the Madison School to establish a small highland school themselves. They were turned from this purpose by the Spirit of Prophecy, which indicated that a training school should first be established near Nashville, and that from this training school workers should go out into highland districts.

Several young people came to the Madison School in its first year who had received some training at Berrien Springs. Among these workers were two young men, Brethren Calvin Kinsman and Orin Wolcott. Both joined the work at Madison with heart and soul, remaining with the institution for one year. At the end of that time they felt convinced that they should go into the island of Cuba as self-supporting missionaries. An effort was made to direct them into some work nearer home, but their minds were settled. They felt that God had called them to Cuba, and so in June 1905, the two young men left Madison for Cuba, going by way of New Orleans. They sold their bicycles to help raise money for transportation, and what they lacked in their own meager funds was made up to then by the little company at Madison. The two young men landed at Havana with less than five dollars between them. They visited Elder Snyder, director of that mission field, whose headquarters at that time were in one of the city's suburbs. They made their expenses for several months by doing carpentry work, in the meantime studying the language. Elder Snyder traveled with them over a part of the island, and on his advice they finally purchased a piece of property. This first property proved to be undesirable land, and later Bro. Kinsman's father invested money in another tract. On this property Cuban buildings were erected. The young men were joined by Christine Owen and Amanda Halverson, Miss Owen becoming Mrs. Kinsman and Miss Halverson Mrs. Wolcott on their arrival in Havana.

This little company of workers, later joined by Miss Bessie Kinsman, conducted a school for several months. When Bro. Kinsman and his wife found it necessary to return to the States because of this health, the work of that little school was continued by a native Cuban and his wife who had been lately brought into the truth through the labors of Bro. Guy Holmes and his wife, and two other students of the Madison School who were carrying on self-supporting mission work near las Menas, in the province of Camaguay. As a result of the work of Bro. Holmes, a church has been organized near this school site, composed of eight or ten Cubans. Bro. Holmes was joined in his work in January 1911 by Bro. Charles Franz and his wife and Sister A. F. Burges, Bro. Franz and his wife were both students of Madison School for some time.

When Professor Sutherland and Mrs. F. C. Gray were on their way home from Cuba in the year 1910, they stopped at Tampa, Florida, where they met a sister of Cuban birth who had spent several years in the States. This sister had been looking for an opportunity to return to Cuba, and was much interested in the self-supporting work. She came to Madison School for a course in the summer school, remained several months in the institution, and accompanied Bro. Franz and his wife to Cuba as a teacher of the Spanish language.

Bro. J. F. Anderson and his wife are conducting a school near Las Tunas, and Sister Ida Fischer-Carnahan has for several years been doing a good work in San Claudio.

When plans were laid at Berrien Springs to begin the work at Madison, there were among the students who volunteered to come south, Bro. Charles Alden and Miss Laura Ashton. These young people were married in the fall of 1904, and joined the Madison school family a little later. Both took their part in the pioneer work of the new institution for about fifteen months. In March 1906, Bro. Alden and Bro. Braden Mulford decided that the time had come for them to establish a school in some highland district. Some time was spent in looking up a site, and finally an option was taken on property seven miles from Goodlettsville, a little town about fifteen miles north of Nashville.

Bro. Alden visited his wife's people in Pittsburgh, and Sister Ashton decided to dispose of her property there and assist the new enterprise. Two-hundred and fifty acres of woodland were purchased. Mr. Mulford, a student of the Madison School, joined Bro. Alden, and they spent a number of weeks living in a little shack on the property. As a result of personal effort with friends and relatives, Bro. Alden's father and mother and five sons joined the school. Sister Ashton's family came south.

Sister Ashton had had years of experience in bakery work in Pennsylvania, and bread-baking became one means by which she won her way into the hearts of the people. She settled in the little log cabin before-referred to after Bro. Alden's house had reached such a stage that he and his wife could move into it. She transformed that log cabin into a habitable house by the use of gunny sacks and whitewash, by repairing the roof, by adding a kitchen, and by making other similar improvements. This was a surprise to the neighbors. She built a Dutch oven on the farm, and the fame of her bread went throughout that region. People have been known to walk miles for the sake of getting a loaf. Sister Ashton is also a nurse, and her daughter was a nurse, and when the neighbors were sick, it was not long until people learned that they were the ones to call in for help.

Bro. Alden cut his way into the woods, cleared land, started an orchard, set out strawberries, purchased a few hens, raised poultry, raised a garden (which surprised the neighbors,) put up a small schoolhouse, and gathered in the children. He is a lover of agriculture, and is famed as a teacher of agricultural subjects. His students became interested, and step by step the little school has grown until at times there have been eighty children in attendance. The little schoolhouse has been crowded to its utmost, and thirty-five of the younger children have been taken into one room of his own home, where Mrs. Alden teaches them.

The blacksmith work, the horseshoeing of the neighborhood, is done at the little school shop by Bro. Charles Ashton, who received his start for this work at the Madison School, to which he came as a 16-year old boy just out of public school. Orchards have been started on various farms in that community. The raising of strawberries has become quite an industry. A public road now runs through the property, where a few years ago was a dense woods.

Mr. Alden is known throughout Sumner County, and at the regular annual teachers' institutes held at Gallatin he is the teacher of agriculture. In the institute conducted for a month in the spring of 1912, 400 students studied agriculture in his classes. Tennessee has a state law that every

125

school in the state shall teach agriculture. For that reason, it is made a regular subject in the teachers' institutes.

Miss Virginia, secretary of the School Improvement Association, met Prof. Alden at one of the annual conventions at Madison, learned of his school in the highlands, visited it, and has become intensely interested in the work he is doing in his community She has done much to extend his influence among the teachers of the county and the state.

Bro. Mulford remained for a few months with Bro. Alden, until it became evident that his work would become a permanent one, there now being five families there. He then went in search of a location for another school. He felt that he was providentially directed to a property near Fountain Head, thirty miles northeast of Nashville. Fountain Head is so named because it divides the headwaters of the tributaries of the Ohio and the Tennessee. Bro. Mulford had no means to put into a school, but he had friends and relatives, and these he interested in the enterprise. He was joined by his sister and her husband, Bro. Forrest West, and by his wife's mother with her family, and among them they raised sufficient funds to purchase . . . . .[1] acres.

This was a worn-out farm, and the experiences of those young people in developing the land, in building up a school, and in changing the spirit of that community has attracted widespread attention among the people of Fountain Head. One of the most striking signs of the growth in this school is seen in the development of their canning business. The preservation of fruit and vegetables is almost unknown in these highland districts. The school purchased a cannery, and in its garden raised beans, tomatoes, and okra. There some fruit on the place, and this was also canned. Gradually the neighbors were encouraged to raise gardens and were given an opportunity to have their goods canned in the school cannery. In the year 1912, that little school plans to can 10,000 quarts of fruit and vegetables. Their tomatoes and string beans have ready sale on the market in Gallatin and Nashville. The products of their cannery go into the homes of the neighbors, who have changed their ideas from raising tobacco alone to

---

[1] This ellipses is found in the original manuscript as written here.

raising a diversified crop, and whose diet has been changed decidedly for the better.

This school draws patronage from some of the best families in and around Fountain Head. Gradually new barns, a workshop, and a cottage or two have been erected, and a number of boarding students are cared for each year. Now plans are developing for the building of small treatment rooms, for it is found that in connection with such a highland school, some provision must be made for the care of the sick. One young lady from the company is taking the nurses' course, preparatory to working in that community. Friends in the North have been interested, and the money for the treatment rooms has been raised. The influence of the school and the good that it is accomplishing cannot be given in a few words. One needs to visit such a community to really appreciate the work.

A church organization has been begun at Fountain Head. There is also a church organization in connection with Bro. Alden's school. In fact, since the Madison School began work in Tennessee, six churches have been formed in Tennessee, besides some outside the state.

Among the pioneers in the highland school work were Bro. Chris Holm and his wife, who came from Idaho, and spent some time as students in the Madison School. Bro. Helm entered this work against the counsel of the teachers at Madison. He had a struggle with poverty, living at first in an old house that was on the place he purchased on Paradise Ridge. The land was extremely poor. Bro. Holm was joined by his brother and wife. Both men were accustomed to working in the woods, and they finally set up a mill. As the work grew, they built a neat bungalow for their own home, the lumber being sawed from the surrounding woods. A schoolhouse, which is a credit to any community, was put up, and school work begin.

Later, this property was sold to Bro. H. D. Meeker and family, from Oregon. Bro. Calkins and his wife conducted the school work while the two Brethren Helm joined their forces to the school enterprise started by Elder C. N. Martin and family, near Bon Aqua, Tenn. This company was also located in a wooded district, and the two Brethren Holms carried on their sawmill work there. This work has grown quietly and steadily, Elder Martin and his wife having done ministerial and missionary work, which has resulted in the organization of a church.

Top: Attendees of the first self supporting workers convention.
Bottom: E. A. Sutherland poses with unknown convention group.

CHAPTER 34

HILLCREST

Before the opening of the Madison School, while the Madison company were still working in Berrien Springs, they had associated with then Bro. O. R. Staines. Bro. Staines connected with the faculty at Huntsville, Ala., and a little later Bro. W. H. Williams, also a Berrien Springs worker, joined the Huntsville folk. After severing his connection with Huntsville, Bro. Staines and his wife spent some time at Madison. His interest in the colored work had been deeply aroused by the Huntsville experience, and he studied the problem carefully, being somewhat puzzled to know how to start a colored school.

At the time the Madison School farm was purchased, Sister White wrote Eld. Daniells as follows:

> We should enter at once upon the establishment in suitable places near Nashville of a school for white people and a school for colored people. . . There are in Nashville large institutions for the education of the colored people, and our colored school is to be near enough to these institutions for the wing of their protection to be thrown over it.

Some counselled the sale of the Huntsville property and the starting of a work at Nashville, but Sister White said the Huntsville School should continue its work where it was, and that a new school for colored workers should he established within easy reach of Nashville. Elder J. E. White and Sister White had talked over this colored school problem, and when the trip up the Cumberland River, it was with the idea of finding a suitable location for a colored training school. Describing the property seen along the river, she said: "We looked at several places, but the fertile land up the river is altogether too high in price for us to think of purchasing it for school purposes."

Bro. Staines determined to search for a place suitable for a training school for colored workers, on which the plan of operation would be similar to the work being conducted at the Madison School. He met the Southern Union Conference Committee (Prof. Sutherland also being present,) at Nashville, and talked about his plans with them, receiving their endorsement.

Then began the search for land. In various ways, it became very evident that the property they purchased on the White's Creek Pike, now known as the Hillcrest Farm, located about five miles from the city of Nashville, was a desirable place for building up a colored school. When, a year later, the Roger Williams College, one of the well-known colored institutions of the South, suffered loss by fire in Nashville and was rebuilt on this same pike within two miles of the Hillcrest Farm, it became still more evident that this was a favorable location for a colored school.

Bro. Staines had but little money with which to start the enterprise, and great faith was required. When the option was taken, it required all the money in the pockets of Bro. Staines and Sutherland. Ten dollars more was required to bind the bargain. Bro. Staines' mother united with his efforts, and together they were able to raise enough money to make the first payment on the place.

Years ago, the Spirit of Prophecy stated,

> The Lord is grieved by the woe in the southern field. Christ has wept at the sight of this woe. Angels have hushed the music of their harps as they have looked upon a people unable to help themselves.

When the Madison work was started, this instruction was given:

> Brethren Sutherland and Magan should be encouraged to solicit means for the support of their work. It is the privilege of these brethren to receive gifts from any of the people whom the Lord impresses to help. They should have means, God's means, with which to work.

This same instruction was applicable to the building up of a training school for colored people. Bro. Staines made a trip through the North, visiting his friends and telling them of the need for such a school. Prof. Floyd Brailiar, then connected with Stuart (Iowa) Academy, decided to join Bro. Staines.

Hillcrest has utilized for school purposes the old farm house that was on the place. For students and teachers, small cottages have been erected on the same general plan as that followed at Madison. These cottages have come as the result of gifts bestowed by friends interested in the colored work. As their work developed, it became evident that a larger amount of land was needed to furnish employment for students. An adjoining farm of ninety-seven acres was purchased. On this farm was a comfortable house, which has been used by teachers and workers; and the money needed to make the payments on this farm has been subscribed by friends of the work.

Hillcrest has made a decided growth. Their principal means of income has been through their nursery. This has also been an avenue through which the influence of Hillcrest has been felt in various quarters in Nashville. Some of the wealthiest families in the city are supplied from this nursery, and Prof. Bralliar is recognized as an authority on landscape gardening and floriculture. This department of the work has furnished employment for colored students. The Hillcrest garden has done well, quite a large amount of canning having been done. A fine grade of poultry has been raised, and the Hillcrest poultry have taken many prizes at the Tennessee State Fair. This has placed the school in a very favorable light.

In nearly every case, colored students need a great deal of help, and the Hillcrest School has to meet problems both educational and financial that sometimes seem more difficult than those to be met with in a white school. Gradually, however, a little company of workers has been prepared to leave the parent school. A man and his wife recently started a small mission school for colored students in Mississippi. A number of Hillcrest students have done good work as canvassers in the city. Some very readable literature has been issued describing Hillcrest work. What has been said in regard to the starting of highland schools gives in general the conditions which have to be met when companies of workers go out. It would be impossible to give a detailed account of the various enterprises, interesting as that matter might be.

Among the school centers that have been established are two on Sand Mountain, a tableland about 100 miles along, in the northern part of the state of Alabama. About twenty miles from the city of Chattanooga, Dr.

O. M. Hayward began a school work in connection with his sanitarium work in the city of Chattanooga.

He found it impossible to do justice to the school work at such a distance, and the property was turned over to Bro. W. R. Tolman and wife and T. A. Graves and family. After working with Bro. Tolman for a time in this school, Bro. Graves established another school near Lawrenceburg, Tenn., and the Old Paths Industrial School is conducted by Bro. Tolman's family, assisted by Miss Lackey and Mrs. McDonald-Waters.

There has always been a strong desire in the minds of these workers to make the school especially strong in the care of orphan children, and this is the direction in which the work is developing. Bro. Graves has been joined at Lawrenceburg by Bro. Geo. Crawford and his wife, who have been laboring in the South for a number of years. Bro. and Sr. Wm. Schlutsmeier are located on property a few miles from Bro. Graves, in another school community, where Sr. Schlutsmeier has been teaching, and where a good work is gradually developing.

Bro. Frank Artress brought his wife south from Washington, D. C., where she had been a student in the Foreign Mission Seminary. They purchased property in Southern Tennessee, seven miles from a railroad, and in a community where educational advantages had always been decidedly limited. In that quiet, out-of-the-way place Bro. and Sr. Artress are laying the foundation for a permanent school. Bro. Artress uses his knowledge of carpentry as a means of supporting himself while at the same time gradually clearing more land and getting his farm into better condition.

The second school on Sand Mountain was started by Bro. Lucian Scott and Bro. and Sr. R. C. Carnahan. Bro. Scott's family assisted in the purchase of the property, and has spent considerable time with the little company. Bro. Scott's wife and mother have largely carried the burden of the school. When times have been hard in this little community, Bro. Scott has canvassed for the sake of bringing in cash.

Bro. H. M. Walen and Bro. Geo. Wallace came south with their families from the state of California. Bro. Wallace had been a teacher of mechanics in Healdsburg College. Sr. Walen was a teacher of considerable experience, and Bro. Walen was a businessman. These two families spent some time at the Madison School, and then the two brethren went out in search of a school site. They located in a rather isolated district northeast of Fountain Head. The two families lived in the one log house on the place for a year; then Bro. Wallace put up a cottage for his family, and the largest room in the old house was remodeled for school purposes. A school with an enrollment of between fifteen and thirty-five children has been held here for several years.

The original members of this company have been assisted in their work by Miss Elisabeth Payne, of Springfield, Mass., by Bro. Harold Matthews of California, who spent one year there preparatory to starting a work of his own, and by Bro. Hershel Ard, who has done an excellent work in the community by holding farmers' conventions. The effects of this work may be seen from the fact that in July 1912, a community meeting was held on the farm of the Fountain Head Industrial School, conducted by Brn. West and Mulford, bringing together the neighbors of the two schools. Several workers in the state and federal departments of agriculture as well as some of our own speakers addressed the assemblage.

Two Ohio ministers, Eld. Geo. Redfield and Eld. W. T. Downing, became deeply interested in the southern work, and with their families located on a property near Portland, Tenn. Those who are familiar with conditions in the South will realize that one needs to go but a few miles from many of the towns and even cities to find himself in an isolated district. And it is in such places that the schools already mentioned have been located. After Bro. Harold Matthews had had one year's experience in the Chestnut Hill Industrial School, he spent the summer at his home in California for the purpose of interesting friends in this cause. In the autumn of 1911, he returned and purchased the property on which Elders Downing and Redfield had been working. He has been joined by Bro. and Sr. Siebert and Bro. and Sr. Lewis of Iowa. So, in a most unostentatious way, the Spring Branch Farm School is beginning its work.

Bro. Bert White, Bro. Ira Woodman, Bro. Geo. Gruesbeck and their families, with Miss Foote, together started a school in the Sequatchie Valley in Eastern Tennessee. This is a picturesque place, reached by a narrow-gauge railroad running up the valley a distance of about 40 miles. Years before, a school had been conducted on the farm which they purchased, so that the name college clung to the place, and in that same college building this company have carried on schoolwork, having as many as 100 children on their roll.

The struggles in any one of these schools over the matter of support is an interesting story. The Spirit of the Lord works upon the hearts of men and women to put practically everything they own into this work. In most cases it will be seen that two or three families unite to start a work. A sufficient amount of money can usually be commanded by those who go into it to purchase the property and to begin a school. In most cases the farm is in such a condition that the soil must be built up gradually. It is a slow process. But while the work is being developed for the outside people, a sturdiness of character is developed in the workers that is often amazing. One cannot help thinking of the expression used in the Spirit of Prophecy:

> The class of education given at the Madison School is such as will be accounted a treasure of great value by those who take up work in foreign fields. If many more in other schools were receiving a similar training, we as a people would be a spectacle to the world, to angels, and to men. The message would be quickly carried to every country, and souls now in darkness would be brought to the light.

Without doubt these little schools are even now a spectacle, not only to men of the world, but to angels in heaven. Their work is guarded and cared for by the Lord Himself. Further, the Spirit of Prophecy says:

> In the work being done at the Madison School, in the work being done at the training school for home and foreign missionary teachers in Madison, Tenn., and in the small schools established the teachers who have gone forth from Madison, we have an illustration of one way in which the message should be carried in many, many places.

When Sister White was talking to a company of teachers from these same little schools, she said, "I am glad that our people are established here at Madison. I am glad to meet these workers here, who are offering themselves to go to different places. God's work is to advance steadily; his truth is to triumph." Further she said to this same company of workers, "We feel an earnest interest in these schools. There is a wide field before us in the establishment of family mission schools."

When it was found that the company in the Sequatchie Valley was strong enough to carry the work without Bro. and Sr. Woodman, they left that place for Alabama. Some time before this, Bro. Clarence Waldron and wife had purchased property and had begun school work near Rockford. Bro. Waldron had been working alone, and his work was decidedly strengthened toy the addition of Bro. Woodman and wife.

Bro. George Leitzman and his wife, who have for years been working in the South, have a school center near Red Level, Ala., in the vicinity of Mobile. Bro. Richard Glatter and his wife, who are especially interested in the development of treatment rooms, but who wish to combine that with educational work for the children, are located near Borden Springs, in Eastern Alabama.

In supplying a list of workers who have given their lives to the development of industrial school work, largely in a self-supporting way, mention should be made of the years of toil given to the southern field by Eld. D. T. Shireman, who established a school at Hildebran. Later this school passed into the hands of Prof. J. W. Beach and Elder Shireman turned his attention to the care of orphans at Toluca and Baker's Mountain. There are also Eld. J. O. Johnston, in his work at Eufola, N. C., and Bro. M. H. Johnston, who has a flourishing school, with a home for aged people and orphans at Baker's Mountain, N. C.; also Prof. C. G. Howell, who has spent many years near McMinnville, Tenn.; Prof. C. L. Kendall and his family, who, on leaving the Madison School, purchased property near Kensett, Ark. for the development of an industrial school.; and Bro. Bert Owen and company, who are located near Sequatepeque, Spanish Honduras. In Bro. Owen's company are Bro. and Sr. Howard Loftin and Sister Lura Davidson, formerly members of the Madison School, and Bro. and Sister Carl Snow, both of whom were associated with the work at Berrien Springs.

There are at the present time (summer of 1912) several companies that have either just located or are about to locate for the purpose of establishing schools. Eld. W. F. Brown, president of the Kentucky Conference, has made several visits to the Madison School, urging young people to visit his conference with a view to locate there. Bro. Bay Beal and wife have purchased property in Kentucky, where Eld. Brown had held meetings and an interest had been awakened. They were compelled to hurry their plans for the development of their school in order to meet the demand of the community for a fall term, to begin in August. Bro. Beal has succeeded in interesting a number of friends and relatives in the North, making it possible for him to have in his company a teaching force, farmers, and one or more mechanics.

Bro. Fred Jacobs and his family have become interested in Kentucky, and have recently purchased property. In January 1912, Bro. and Sr. E. W. Hurlbutt of California came south for the second time. They had been interested in the Madison work for several years, and had at one time visited the school. They spent about three months in Northern Georgia in search of a suitable place for the development of a school work. In March they purchased a 400-acre tract near Reeves. Here they hope to gather together a company of workers for the purpose of developing a school and small sanitarium.

Prof. H. B. Allen and Eld. W. E. Videto, with R. H. Gilman and R. B. King, all of Michigan, are united in the development of an industrial school near Leatherman, N. C. The work here is in a way unique, because the buildings are erected and other financial problems are met by the sale of the Mountain School Herald, a little paper published in the interests of that work by Bro. Allen.

Prof. Brownsberger and his wife are located at a most desirable site at Naples, N. C., fifteen miles from Asheville.

CHAPTER 35

LOCAL CONVENTIONS

An interesting work in connection with the small schools is the local conventions they hold. To illustrate, there are three schools within easy reach of Fountain Head, and the teachers from these schools hold quarterly meetings. At these meetings they make a study of the problems to be met in those particular schools. It is usually possible for them to have some outside help, and these local conventions have proved of special benefit in the development and strengthening of their schools. In several places the neighbors have been interested through these conferences.

Considerable enthusiasm has been aroused over contests for the raising of particular crops. The agricultural men of the state have become interested in the work done in a number of the highland schools, as is evinced by the meeting held at Fountain Head on July 12, which was attended by a number of these workers.

Perhaps the first conference of this sort was called by Prof. Alden in connection with his school work at Goodlettsville, in the summer of 1909. Gradually his influence as a teacher of agriculture and as an authority on certain agricultural subjects has been extended through his association with the normal institutes of Middle Tennessee, and with Miss Virginia Moors in her work in the School Improvement Association.

The religious work in these school centers is made prominent from the first. In many instances, the first contact with the people has come through Sunday School work and attending the district prayer meetings. The little schoolhouse becomes a center for Sunday evening meetings, as well as for Sabbath Schools and Sunday Schools.

It is not an unusual thing for the school workers to be given a leading part in the neighborhood Sunday Schools. Regular Sunday evening services are frequently conducted, and many times the attendance from the neighborhood is surprisingly large. A large amount of literature has been distributed in certain communities. There is something about the work that makes the teachers lean heavily on the Lord, and one who visits these schools is usually impressed with both the mental and the spiritual activity of the workers.

CHAPTER 36

DEPARTMENT MEETINGS

In addition to the regular class work of the institution, the Union Meetings are considered a decidedly educational feature. The work of the entire school is kept before the student body through these Union Meetings, reports being brought into three meetings from practically every department of the school.

For instance, the dairy, the orchard, the farm, the garden, the poultry, the goats, the teams, the fence and repair work, the shop work, and the work of the carpentry department are all reported to the Union Body through the weekly report from the men's meeting, while a similar report comes in from the sanitarium and another one from the women's department. The men hold a weekly meeting for the consideration of their work. The women hold a similar meeting, and the sanitarium workers have their department meetings. At these meetings, a chairman presides and a secretary keeps record of the proceedings. The reports of the work done in each department is rendered to the Union Body by the secretary of the department.

Each department has its plans and Inspection Committee, whose duty it is to suggest lines of work that should be done and to suggest improvements along all lines. Rooms are inspected, and students are expected to keep their rooms and the grounds surrounding their cottages subject to inspection. A general system of reporting irregularities in work and attending meetings is followed. An irregularity in work may subject the individual to an assessment.

For instance, a young man drives through a gate and leaves it open; he is subject to an assessment, the amount being settled by the vote of the department. Sometimes it is argued that he should not be assessed. Then the question is raised: if he leaves the gate open and the cattle come into the garden and destroy $25 worth of garden produce, will he pay for the damage done? Or a driver allows his horse to stand without tying. He may do so ten times and no harm come, but once when he does it the horse becomes frightened, and the buggy is broken, possibly the horse itself is injured; will he pay for the damage done? When students confront such propositions as this, they usually decide that it is wiser to put themselves in a place where they guard against accidents by assessing themselves a reasonable amount, such as ten cents, or from this on up to a dollar or a dollar and a half, rather than, by laxness in discipline, be in danger of a much heavier expense through an accident. Irregularities such as attendance at class or at chapel service are handled by the body itself. There are certain things which are deemed excusable; there are certain other things which it may be lawful for a student to do but for which he is not expected to give an excuse. Once a week he is given an opportunity to state his irregularities and to give the reasons. A record of these irregularities appears on the student's term report.

CHAPTER 37

RELIGIOUS INFLUENCE

In considering the religious phase of the work, something should be said. A strong religious atmosphere permeates the work. The Bible is taught constantly. The Spirit of Prophecy is studied as a basis for the development of practically every department of the work. Worship is conducted twice each day, and every member of the family is expected to be in attendance. Sabbath services usually consist of a social meeting Sabbath evening, Sabbath School and a preaching service Sabbath morning, a meeting of some nature usually on Sabbath afternoon, and during a large part of the year a service with the sanitarium patients at the close of the Sabbath. Wednesday evening of each week the students have a prayer meeting. At this hour it has been the custom for the past two years to make a study of the South and its needs a leading topic. Prayer is offered for those who are interested in the South or who should be interested. Letters are read by students and teachers from those who are in the work or who are preparing to enter the work. Reports are given by those who are out in the canvassing field, or from those who have been working in Nashville, and who are home for the day.

Students also have, once each week, division meetings for prayer and study, and at these little meetings some of the most interesting personal experiences have been gained. From the time the school was established, work of various kinds has been done in the community. There are three or four churches within walking distance of the school, and both students and teachers have had part in the Sunday School work in these churches. For months at a time, teachers and students have united in carrying on the work of a Sunday School near the ferry in Neeley's Bend. It was a canvasser from the school in its early days who found a Sabbath-keeper who had been brought into the truth through reading, but was not acquainted with any other Sabbath-keepers. She became a member of the Madison Church when it was organized. Little companies of students have held Bible readings in various families. Companies of canvassers have worked in the city of Nashville at various times, and in the spring of 1912 a number of students took up the canvassing work in Nashville. When a campaign for the sale of Ministry of Healing was organized for the benefit of the sanitarium, the Madison Church was the first to dispose of its quota of books for the benefit of the Nashville Sanitarium. Students have entered heartily into the canvassing for special numbers of the Signs and the Review and Herald. One line of missionary work which has proved beneficial to the young people has been the writing of missionary letters to the young people's societies in their home churches, for the purpose of interesting them in the South. Considerable literature has been put into the hands of our own people in this way.

CHAPTER 38

BEGINNING OF SCHOOL WORK

In 1904, the company settled on the Madison School farm never lost sight of the fact that it was their purpose to develop a school. The matter of support was important, but the development of the school was of greater importance, and the first winter on the farm saw a short term of school. During the following spring, a still longer term was conducted, and while the number of students was limited, regular class work was conducted. It has been said that the success of a school does not depend upon fine buildings and extensive paraphernalia. The school work in Madison began under great difficulties. For a year, one of the low, dark rooms in Old Plantation House was chapel and dining room, and between meals the tables in the dining room would be pushed back into the corners and the room used for recitation purposes. The front hallway contained a bed, and two young men slept there. The first nurses' class was taught by Mrs. Druillard. This was before the sanitarium was built, and before there were any patients on the place, and their practical demonstrations of massage and hydrotherapeutic treatments were given in one of the bedrooms on the second floor of Old Plantation. The water for fomentations was heated in a pail on a little airtight stove. A board on two wooden horses was the treatment table, and with those meager facilities that first class received its training. Three of the six members are now professional nurses. One of them is head nurse of our own sanitarium. Another is supporting an aged mother and father by her work. This shows that efficient work was done in that class.

The work done by the institution's bookkeeper is usually considered decidedly interesting by those who investigate the workings of the institution. The school has been blessed by having as business manager and bookkeeper a woman of unusual experience, and one who has worked in various large institutions. It is the custom here to keep a book account with every department of the institution. It is known just how many hours each student spends in working in each department. The exact running expense and the exact income of each department is known. The bookkeeper of the institution is the one who teaches the classes in bookkeeping, and it can readily be seen that she is able to give her students a more practical line of work. In fact, the classes in bookkeeping are carried through a course practically embodying the work on the institution's books—time reports, bills, department reports, expenditures, the running of the boarding department, the putting up of buildings, etc., form the basis for their entries. A number of young people have in this way developed into skillful bookkeepers.

CHAPTER 39

THE ROAD

One complaint made by those who opposed the purchase of the Madison farm was that it was too far from the city of Nashville for any reasonable connection to be maintained with city work, and the road from Gallatin Pike to the farm was in such poor condition that for sanitarium purposes, at least, the trip presented an obstacle too great for patients. In coming from Madison Station, the hardest part of the trip lay along the road which bordered the school farm on the west. This was known as the Larkin Springs Lane. It was a rocky road, demanding constant repair because of the steepness of its hills. From this road, there was another hard pull for teams hauling loads up to the sanitarium or the school buildings.

In the fall of 1905, a committee was appointed to study the question of roads, and at that time a road was proposed across the school grounds which would cut out the Larkins Springs Lane altogether. But in those days the building of a road was entirely beyond the reasonable venture of the school. Not until the year 1910 did the way open for active work to be done on the road.

As the sanitarium grew, it became absolutely necessary to make it easier to reach that institution. After careful study of the situation, it was decided to build a macadamized road twelve feet wide from the sanitarium, extending over the highest part of the property, near the water tower, and joining the Neeley's Bend Road on the south.

The general oversight of making this road was put into the hands a of the County Roadmaster, Squire Menese. The stone for these roads was taken from some of the older stone walls on the place. Some was gathered from rocky fields. This stone was crushed to make a graded roadbed. Mr.

Menese employed some the neighbors on this work, and the school furnished some help in the way of men and teams. The rock was crushed on the piece by a machine. Before the school had completed its road, arrangements were made by the county to place the chain-gang on the Neeley's Bend Road. During the winter of 1911-12, this gang worked this road from Gallatin Pike to the river, cutting down the hills, filling up the low places, and making the Neeley's Bend Road equal to Gallatin Pike. With these improvements, the trip from Nashville to the sanitarium has been made a very desirable one, and patients and their friends in the city are within easy reach of one another. The one and only thing that made the farm seem too far from Nashville has in the course of a few years been entirely removed.

During the same time, the plans for extending the trolley car line from Nashville to Gallatin have been perfected, and within a few months the interurban will give services between these two points. On the farm, there is about a mile and a half of road, at a cost of about $1500. The road, as other improvements, was made possible by the gifts of friends interested in the development of this work.

CHAPTER 40

ORGANIZATION

T he Madison School farm, the buildings thereon, the cattle, the machinery, and all other personal property, of whatever name and nature, are the property of a legal corporation, "The Nashville Agricultural and Normal Institute." No property of any name or nature is held individually by or in the name of any trustee or person.

This corporation is organized under what is generally known as the "General Welfare Act" of the state of Tennessee. This is the one act which provides for the legal ownership of schools, colleges, hospitals, sanitariums, benevolent associations, churches, etc. in the state.

This act provides that the property of this corporation becomes to all intents and purposes a gift forever to the purpose for which the institution is founded. There is no way known to the law by which the founders, the trustees, or the operators of the institution can ever alienate the property from the purpose stated in the charter. There is no way known to the law by which the founders, the trustees, or the constituents can in any way bring the corporation to an end and distribute the property among the donors or any other persons.

More particularly stated, the objects of this corporation are the establishment and maintenance of a training school in the state of Tennessee and county of Davidson, the work of which shall be the training of ministers of the gospel, evangelists, missionary teachers, and missionary farmers, who shall have in mind to devote a part or all of their lives to the service of God and the betterment of humanity. It is denominational and sectarian to the extent that it shall always teach and inculcate the doctrines and tenets of the Seventh-day Adventist faith.

The law provides for the number of trustees, the calling of meetings, the officers and their duties.

It stipulates that if at any time the members of the society shall desire to turn over the entire property to another corporation, they can do so, provided, that such corporation is qualified to carry money and property in trust along the same lines and with the same objects as held by the founders of the concern.

An arrangement was also made in the By-Laws, whereby persons who have donated $25 or more to the institution, may, if they so desire, have some voice in the management thereof. Provision was made for a board of managers to arrange for the conduct of the institution. Each person giving $25 to the institution has the right to vote for this board of managers. This board of managers consists of fifteen persons. The present board includes a number of representative men of the Southern Union Conference Committee.

The principal features of the charter of the Madison school and of the Act under which the charter is drawn, are set forth in a letter written by Mr. A.P. Whitman, of Nashville, Tenn., who has acted as attorney for our denominational corporations at Nashville. This letter, which was addressed to Elder W. C. White is as follows:

Nashville, Tenn. Oct. 31, 1907
Eld. W. C. White,
Sanitarium, Napa Co., Cal.

My dear Sir:

I received a letter from Prof. Percy T. Magan, of Oct. 22, 1907, propounding to me six questions relative to the Nashville Agricultural and Normal Institute, and I was requested to address my reply to you. I presume you have a copy of Professor Magan's letter to me, embracing the six questions, and it will not be necessary for me to set forth the questions in haec verba, but merely to refer to them.

It is proper to state in advance that all corporations chartered or organized in this state which are not for profit or money-making on the part of those interested, such as churches, colleges, schools, religious organizations, missionary associations, fraternities, fairs, parks, and so forth, all fall under the article of our code under the heading of "Corporations for the General Welfare and not for Profit." All such corporations are governed by the same law. In such corporations there is no capital stock, and, therefore, there are no stockholders; the members of such corporations are as so many individuals, each having one vote in the management and control of its affairs. The property of the corporation is vested in the corporate entity, and no individual member as such has any pecuniary interest in the property. Therefore no member can give, sell, bequeath, or devise to any other person any part of said corporation, nor upon the death of a member does there any interest in the corporation descend to his heirs at law, or next of kin. With this preface I can perhaps answer your questions more satisfactorily.

1) Is the Nashville Agricultural and Normal Institute in any sense whatsoever the private property of Edward A. Sutherland, Nellie H. Druillard, M. Bessie DeGraw, P. T. Magan, or of the other incorporators, Mrs. Ellen G. White, Elder S. N. Haskell, and Eld. George I. Butler, each and any or all of them? Is it not a fact that this corporation is organized under the General Welfare Act of the State of Tennessee, under which almost all schools, churches, hospitals, and benevolent associations of every name and nature are organized?

Answer. The property of the Nashville Agricultural and Normal Institute is in no sense the private property of anyone. To the second clause of the question I would answer: yes, all such institutions are chartered under the same statute. The Southern Union Conference of Seventh-day Adventists, and all other associations of like nature chartered in this State since the act of 1875 (the year of the passage of the General Welfare Act) have been chartered under this law.

2) Under the terms and provisions of the General Welfare Act of the State of Tennessee, is it possible for any individual to have any personal property interest of any name or nature in a corporation formed under the terms ad provisions of that Act? Can any member of such a corporation, sell, bequeath, or assign his interest in such corporation to any other individual, the same as he would any piece of real or personal property?

Answer. No; there is no way by which one can transfer an individual interest in the corporation; the property is in no way divisible so as to separate a part from the whole. To the second clause of this question, I answer; No, as clearly indicated above.

3) In particular, have Nellie Druillard, Edward A. Sutherland, Percy T. Magan, M. Bessie DeGraw, et. al., any special interest in the Nashville Agricultural and Normal Institute; have they any lien against its property?

Answer. Neither of the parties named has any individual interest in said property, nor have they any lien upon any part of it

4) Is the farm property which was purchased from W. B. Ferguson and his wife, Sarah E. Ferguson, in Neeley s Bend, the Old Nineteenth Civil District, Madison, Davidson Co., Tennessee, held in the name of the Nashville Agricultural and Normal Institute; and is it deeded to them, or is it the property of the above-named individuals

Answer. I have examined the deed to the property formerly owned by W. B. Ferguson and wife, mentioned in this question, and find that the deed to the property was duly executed by S. N. Haskell and wife to the Nashville Agricultural and Normal Institute on the 4th day of August 1905, and the same is recorded in Book 318, page 74, of the Register1s Office in this county, which is the proper office for the registration of such conveyance. I have examined the office from the making of the deed by Ferguson and wife down to the present and find that there are no liens or mortgages of any kind on said property; an absolute title is vested in the Nashville Agricultural and Normal Institute.

5) Under the terms and provisions of the General Welfare Act, is any individual member of a corporation authorized under that act more than one vote in the affairs of such corporation; in other words, can a corporation formed under the aforesaid act be in any sense a stockholder's corporation?)

Answer. No; nor can any individual member be given or be allowed more than one vote under the law regulating such corporation in this state—the law forbids it.

6) Under the terms and provisions of the General Welfare Act can a corporation authorized under it pay or distribute profits or dividends of any name or nature to any member of said corporation?

Answer. No: any distribution of profits or dividends to any individual would be a diversion of the property of the corporation, and any member would have the right to resort to the courts and compel the return of the same to the corporation. An act of this kind on the part of the member, if not embezzlement, would certainly be a breach of duty on the part of the officials in control of the corporate interests.

Trusting that I have in this brief reply covered the several points upon which you desire information, I am.

Yours very truly,

A. F. Whitman

———————

During the fourth biennial session of the Southern Union Conference, held at Nashville, Tenn., Jan. 9 to 19, 1908, a committee, consisting of Elder K. C. Russell, Judge Cyrus Simmons, and Mr. W. A. Wilcox was appointed to investigate the charter and ownership of the Nashville Agricultural and Normal Institute, This committee submitted the following report:

Your committee appointed to investigate the nature and condition of the Charter granted to the Nashville Agricultural and Normal Institute by the State of Tennessee, respectfully reports as follows;

1. That said charter has been granted under the General Welfare laws of the State of Tennessee, and is for the general welfare of society, and not for individual profit. That none of the members of this corporation are stockholders.

2. That all the moneys and properties owned by said corporation belong to the corporation, and not to the incorporators or to the Board of Directors.

That the incorporators of this concern are constituted by law the first Board of Directors for the purpose of the management of the concern. In the event of the death of these incorporators, the constituency of the corporation have the right to elect another Board of Directors for the purpose of managing the institution. No properties or moneys belonging to the corporation can in any way descend to the heirs or representatives of the incorporators in the event of death. This corporation is organized for educational and religious purposes, teaching the doctrines of the Seventh-day Adventist Church. The properties end moneys belonging to the corporation must be used for the purposes for which the institution was organized. In the event the Board of Directors misapply any of the moneys, or misdirect the use of any of the property belonging to the said corporation, any member of the Seventh-day Adventist Church would have a right to bring the matter before the court, and to have the operation of the institution reviewed and regulated by the orders of the court, so that the corporation shall fulfil the purpose for which it was organized.

3. The deed from S. N. Haskell to the corporation is a warranty-deed, conveying a fee simple title to the corporation, and contains general covenants of warranty.

The charter is so formed by the law of the state of Tennessee, that no incorporator has any individual interest in any of the property of the corporation.

4. We have heard or read, the statements of A. F. Whitman, attorney-at-law of the Nashville bar, and we pronounce his interpretation of the law to be correct.

All of which is respectfully submitted,

Cyrus Simmons, K. C. Russell, W. C. Wilcox,

Committee.